Carey

The life and times of two pioneer Baptist missionaries in China

To All the Raburn
love Britt Towery

by

Britt Towery

The Tao Foundation Missionary Heritage Series
Waco, Texas, USA
2000

Also by Britt Towery

CHRISTIANITY IN TODAY'S CHINA. 2000
1stBooks.com publisher, ISBN 1-58721-410-5

LAO SHE, CHINA'S MASTER STORYTELLER
Tao Foundation Publication, 1999, ISBN 0-9678811-0-2

BAPTISTS AROUND THE WORLD, Albert W. Warden, Editor
(section on China). Broadman & Holman Publishers, 1995

THE CHURCHES OF CHINA,
Taking Root Downward, Bearing Fruit Upward
Baylor University, 1990. (And a German edition, 1987)

THE PENGLAI-PINGDU BAPTIST MEMORIALS
Stories of Southern Baptist pioneers in Shandong China.
Long Dragon Books, Hong Kong, 1989

PATTERNS: Devotions from life
(coauthor with Jody Towery)
Long Dragon Books, Hong Kong, 1986

A BIBLE OUTLINE: The New Testament
(coauthor with Peter Tong). Hong Kong, 1975

EVERYONE PREACHING CHRIST, by Princeton S. Hsu
(translated by Britt Towery). Hong Kong, 1968

Carey Daniel's China Jewel
Tao Foundation Missionary Heritage Series

ISBN: 0-9678811-2-9

Published by:
The Tao Foundation
P.O. Box 656
Hewitt, Texas, 76643
U. S. A.

Internet: <www.laotao.org>

All proceeds from the sale of this book go to Tao Foundation projects, sharing with the Western world insights into the lands and peoples of Asia. Seeking to further a greater mutual appreciation and understanding of Asian cultures, religions and peoples.

The Tao Foundatrion is a non-profit corporation registerd with the Secretary of State of the State of Texas, U. S. A.
Charter Number: 00433040-01
Tax ID: 174-197.0667

Contents

Governor William P. "Bill" Daniel, Carey Daniel's nephew

The Baylor University campus when Carey and Jewell were residents.

Foreword

by

Governor William P. "Bill" Daniel,

Attorney and General Land Agent, Baylor University Trusts

Former Governor of Guam and nephew of Carey Daniel

When our dear Lord lists His "heroes" in the Baptist family of my paragon Grandfather, **Rev. George Mayfield Daniel**, the top name in my opinion will surely be his fifth child, **"Uncle Carey"**! On the same list right opposite his name under "heroines" could easily be Uncle Carey's admirable wife, our dear "Aunt Jewell."

And somewhere in God's proud description of Uncle Carey, who would have qualified easily as His thirteenth Apostle, the Lord will probably use such exemplary nouns as: Christian; Preacher; Missionary; Evangelist; Puritan; moralist; author; scholar; linguist; husband; father; historian; Mason; poet; cavalier; horseman; and more. No doubt our Lord's adjectives for him will include: Godly; Christlike; celestial; faithful; dedicated; fearless; excelling; impeccable; humble and on and on. Because in fact, he was all that and much more!

In addition, Uncle Carey, whom I have so proudly revered all my life, was an honor graduate of Baylor University in Waco, Texas and the Southern Baptist Theological Seminary in Louisville, Kentucky. As a popular, foremost campus leader, he excelled academically and as a forensic orator and star debater, all the while pastoring several different Baptist churches in Hill County, Texas and elsewhere within a 50-mile proximity to Waco and Louisville.

Since my earliest recall of Uncle Carey for these nearly 84 years, I've lived in fantasy-awe, sympathetic admiration and poignant emulation of this role model for me. Regrettable, her missionary absences and other unavoidable logistics denied me the privilege of knowing Aunt Jewell better. My extensive archival collections of his diaries, photographs, letters, books,

1

clippings, sermons, poetry, correspondence with his adored brother who was my father, Marion Price Daniel, Sr., are among my most treasured family possessions.

These priceless jewels I have guarded carefully with a relentless hope and dream that someday my long sought biographical compilation about dear Uncle Carey and Aunt Jewell's lives of Christian ministry would be properly recorded. Although I do not personally know the author, Britt Towery, my gratitude, ardent prayers and unremitting hope for God's richest blessings go out to him, particularly in his efforts with this historical biography. His asking me to write this preface to his book is a signal honor.

Especially how appropriate it is to emphasize their nonpareil renditions on this Continent as well as those happy, climatic years while Foreign Missionaries in their cherished China. For it was there he discipled so exemplary of our dear Lord and made the supreme sacrifice in giving his young life to his beloved God, Church, Family and Baylor. This shocking tragedy resulted when he was swept from his faithful white horse and drowned in a swollen stream while returning home after a 3-day evangelical mission which destined his immortal bones to lie even yet in an unknown grave.

Indeed, Uncle Carey knew the love of Jesus, the pain of Job, the sacrifice of Paul, the joy of Joseph and Mary and the unremitting Christian influence of his own consecrated Earthly pastor-Father and our distinguished pastor-Great-Grandfather, Rev. Allen Lowery. Also, that of his indomitable Mother, devoted Wife and their fellow-colleagues with whom they worked and served in China, like the celebrated Miss Lottie Moon and others.

It is my unalterable, fervent prayer that God will increase His most meaningful, evangelical icons on Earth like Uncle Carey Daniel and Aunt Jewell Daniel.

Respectfully,

Governor Bill Daniel
Liberty, Texas
September 30, 1999

2

Carey Daniel and Jewell Legett Daniel
Pioneer Baptist Missionaries to China

Introduction

"To be ignorant of what occurred before you were born is to remain a child. For what is the worth of human life unless it is woven into the life of our ancestors by the records of history?"
—— Cicero, Roman orator.

With every trip my wife and I made to the China mainland from 1982 to 1999, and the time we lived there (1989), I was made aware of the vast differences in East and West. We lived in Asian settings (cities and villages) for nearly forty years. In that time it became evident to us that our world is made up of many worlds. Worlds of people few of us know anything about apart from inadequate newspaper reports and the usual stereotypes.

Reading books, seeing documentary films, even visiting other lands does not adequately get us in touch with people of other languages and cultures. One has to be immersed in the village or town or area from as early an age as possible. The earlier that immersion comes of a knowledge of the customs, society and local language is to the advantage.

That is the reason children born in China of missionaries, commercial business people or State Department officials had a head start over the rest of us in language school and grasp of the society.

The early missionaries to China attempted almost the impossible. In the 19th century missionaries left America with no intention of returning. Many never returned, women more than men, due to death in childbirth. Many missionary mothers and wives lie buried across China, most in graves that have given way to urban renewal and growth of cities where none existed a century ago.

This introduction is not intended to do more than what an introduction does: present something that may be new or unknown, or not too well-known, to the Western reader. Besides introducing Carey and Jewell Legett Daniel is the desire to encourage more intense research and renewed respect of the Baptist missionary heritage.

A word about Shandong province

China's Shandong province has a recorded history longer than most parts of China. It was here that Confucius (551-479 B.C.) was born and died. This greatest of all China's sages wandered these barren hills and fruitful valleys, teaching an ethic and standard of life few rulers appreciated. Five hundred years before Christ uttered the Golden Rule (do unto others as you would have them do unto you) Confucius was on the same wave length, only in the negative (don't do to others what you don't want them to do to you).

The famous First Emperor of China, Qin Shi Huang Di, who founded the Qin dynasty (221-207 B.C.) and conceived the idea of linking the northern border fortresses into the Great Wall. He was the emperor who ordered the construction of the now famous terricotta soldiers outside the city of Xi'an. He once visited Shandong (long before it had that name) seeking the elixir of life. Instead of finding the fountain of youth, he died in Shandong. Today the province covers 58,000 square miles with the longest shoreline of any China province. Today it is home to nearly 80 million people. One of China's most cherish classics, (*Shui hu zhuan* - "Outlaws of the Marsh") came from events in Shandong during the Spring and Autumn Period (770-476 B.C.).

Towering in the middle of the province and stretching to the sea is the magnificent range of mountains known all over China as "Mt. Tai." Great Tang poets have claimed that when looking around the top of Mt. Tai, all eight corners under the sky are in view.

Revolts against the throne were common in Shandong. Such as the 17th century revolts against the coming of the Manchus to power. These and other classics are some of China's most treasured literature. Still in demand today are books like "Shui Hu Zhuan" (translated by Pearl Buck as "All Men Are Brothers") and the "Romance of the Three Kingdoms."

4

More recent events

German and Japanese "colonies" controlled some areas of the province toward the end of the 19th and first half of the 20th centuries. From 1877-1918 the Germans turned the ancient fishing village into the present city of Qingdao. The city is better know by an older spelling: Ching Tao, the brand of beer now world famous.

When Germany was defeated in World War I the Japanese gained control of the area and held most of it until the end of World War II in 1945.

There were many famines in this land of wheat, sweet potatoes and maize. Cotton, peanuts and tobacco have been the main cash crops. The history of Shandong famines and the hearty, honest peasant farmers partly inspired Pearl Buck's book, "The Good Earth." No Chinese writer has ever won a Nobel Prize for fiction but this book *about* China (as Pearl Buck saw it), did.

The Boxer Rebellion of 1900 was an anti-foreign, anti-Christian peasant uprising that had its beginning in northern Shandong province. Those taking part were mostly poor peasants who practiced a type of martial arts that gave the movement the name "boxer." The uprising caused the "siege" of the foreign legations in Beijing that ended with the Western military forces capturing the city and causing the Empress Cixi and her court to flee to Xi'an. Thousands of Chinese Christians died and hundreds of foreign missionaries were killed.

Though there were antimissionary outbreaks in all eighteen provinces during the 1890s the most violent reprisals against Chinese converts and missionaries were in Shanxi and Shandong.

The Shandong Baptist Memorials:

There are a number of monuments to Baptist pioneers in Shandong. In the front of the Monument Street Church in Penglai (called Dengzhou in mid 1850s) is the four-foot tall four-sided monument to Lottie Moon. It was put up soon after her death in 1912 by the members of the church. It was damaged by the Red Guards during the early years of the

Cultural Revolution (1966-76) but has been restored to its original site. Other monuments are to Martha Foster Crawford, James Landrum Holmes and a medical missionary William H. Sears and his colleague, Pastor Li Shouting.

In the foyer of the Monument Street Church is a plaque honoring Martha Foster Crawford. Her husband, T. P. Crawford, was instrumental in building the church in the late 1860s. This marble plaque tells of her ministry in China and was donated by her students and church members in 1911.

Somewhere in a village between Penglai and Yan'tai there was a monument to James Landrum Holmes. Bryan Glass, son of Baptist missionary W. B. Glass, told me he saw it once as a schoolboy on a trip to his CIM school in Yan'tai. James Landrum Holmes and his wife, Sallie Little, were the first resident Southern Baptist missionaries in Shandong. They came to China in 1858 and to Shandong in 1860. He was killed by bandits while trying to negotiate them away from the town.

South of Penglai in the city of Pingdu, the William H. Sears headstone is in the local museum. It is more than just a headstone, it is almost five feet tall and outlines Mr. Sears' work in historical and poetic fashion. It was placed as his tombstone on the grounds of the Oxner Memorial Baptist Hospital in 1923 and shows signs of having been moved several times.

After the horrors of the Boxer Rebellion (1900) the people put up a monument to Pastor Li Shouting. He was the first pastor of the Shaling Baptist Church outside the city of Pingdu. The church's cornerstone has been preserved and one day may be a part of a new church building. Records reveal that Pastor Li baptized more converts than anyone else in China. He carried scars on his back because he would not deny his Lord during the fearful days of 1900 when the Boxers were running rampant in his area. At the time of his death, December 13, 1937, the stone was still standing. It is not known if it still exists. Pingdu County has a Christian heritage that is still very much alive as China enters the 21st century.

Baptist missionary pioneers in Shandong

After her husband's death Sallie Little Holmes stayed on in China for thirty years. J. B. Hartwell and his three wives (he was twice a widower) and three of his children served in Shandong. T. P. Crawford, husband of the more beloved Martha Foster, and J. B. Hartwell seldom agreed on anything. Often Lottie Moon mediated between them and showed more common sense than either of them combined. The best record of those years can be found in the book "Our Ordered Lives Confess" (American-East Asian Relations Series: No. 8), by Irwin T. Hyatt, Jr.

Edmonia Harris Moon arrived in China before her more famous sister but stayed on a few years. C. W. Pruitt of Georgia and wife Ida met on the ship going to China. After her death he married Presbyterian Anna Seward and they named their daughter after his first wife. Ida Pruitt grew up to be an outstanding social worker in Beijing and writer. Her books "A Daughter of Han" and "Old Madam Yin" have been re-issued by Stanford University Press. Ida was also the favorite translator for the famous Chinese storyteller, Lao She (1899-1966).

Dr. T. W. Ayers along with his wife Minnie Skelton were Southern Baptists' first medical workers in North China. He began the Warren Memorial Baptist Hospital in Huangxian in 1903.

John Willim Lowe and his wife Margaret Savage Lowe; Fannie Knight who became Mrs. W. D. King; David Wells Herring and his Australian wife Maggie Nutt; Florence Jones, a nurse and friend of Jewell and Carey; the George P. Bosticks; William Carey Newtons and Dr. and Mrs. James M. Oxner are a few of the 19th century pioneers to North China.

As the 20th century dawned Wiley B. Glass and his wife Eunice Taylor and his second wife Jessie Pettigrew helped put down roots that continue to bear fruit. Edgar L. Morgan and wife Lelah May Carter are primarily remembered for his work in publications. Others appear during the years Carey and Jewell were in China. Jewell Legett and Carey Daniel did not have a long ministry in China, but they had a very meaningful one.

A Word About Chinese Religions

In China there has always been a relative lack of protracted struggle between religion and the state. This historical situation developed because secular political power held undisputed supremacy over religion. Religious organizations were permitted to exist only when they served the political ends of the ruling groups or at least did not threaten hierarchical security. In most cases Confucian rulers had no quarrel with religions, especially when the religions enhanced Confucian values.

Any unlicensed religious organization was regarded with suspicion and antagonism by the governments. Since it was extremely difficult to obtain official approval for new religious movements, the suppression policy produced secret or semisecret practices in almost all religious organizations outside the officially recognized monasteries.

Such a relationship between religion and state continues down to the present day. An example can be seen in the 1966-76 Cultural Revolution period when the Communist government closed all churches, causing many faithful to begin low profile, even secret, meetings.

From time to time there have been movements against religious groups, the persecutions of the year 845 was most notable. Many Nestorian Christians fled north to Mongolia and flourished there even to the time of Ghengis Khan (1162?-1227), a brutal leader who did not persecute religions.

The *San Jiao* — the three teachings

China's history cannot be written without reference, however small, to the *San Jiao* — literally the Three Teachings. Namely: Daoism (Taoism), Buddhism and Confucianism. Though this section deals with Chinese religions, *san jiao*, should not be translated "three religions," but is used to designate "religion." *San jiao* is more properly the three basic teaching groups of China. My friend, Erich Kwong, Hong Kong Baptist Seminary professor, reminds me that etymologically, the English term "religion" is derived from the Latin word *religare*, "to bind." The meaning of *jiao* has no etymological implications about relationships

8

between humans and gods. It has evolved in Chinese to signify a body of doctrines or practices.

On the practical level the three religions that we call the san jiao have meshed into one. To be a good Chinese and fulfill the social responsibilities of a good Confucian one should read the Daoist scripture and offer prayers with the family in the Buddhist temples. There is no thought of religious denominations among the masses of worshippers in modern times.

Daoism.

Daoism is China's only indeginious religion and evolved into a state religion during the Han dynasty. The worship of a pantheon of deities in the human spirit and in the universe. Many ceremonies were conducted on a regular basis by the emperors for the imperial ancestors and gods of the fields. Other ceremonies involved sacrifices for the sun and moon and for lesser dieties such as patron saints of the trades and various spirits of the earth and cosmos. The Daoist (Taoist) preferred to take refuge in a philosophy of passivity expressed in the term wuwei which means "action by inaction or effortlessness". (See Henri Maspero's *Taoism and Chinese Religion*, University of Massachusetts Press, 1981.)

Lao Tzu is said to be the founder and his book *Dao De Jing* (*Tao te ching*) is the source of their doctrines. A book that is difficult to interpret and understand even by many Chinese.

Translations of these "scriptures" into the world's languages has generally only added to the confusion of what is primary and basic in Daoist's beliefs and understanding of life.

Confucianism.

China's greatest sage, Confucius, has already been noted. He was born in present-day Shandong province in 551 BC. He traveled the country stressing the need for good government and the importance of good relations between emperor and people. The Confucian systems have been the primary repositories of ethical wisdom. Being regarded by emperors

9

as being necessary to daily life and happiness.

Confucian schools of ethics, morals, philosophy and religion were and are without number. Many represent moral values and human order needing to blend with the cosmic order. Confucian concepts evolved through a hierarchy based on superior-inferior relationships.

Through the centuries the works of Confucius ("The Four Books" and "The Five Classics") have developed thousands of commentaries which eventually became the basis for the civil service examinations. (See Zhang Desheng's book, *Confucian Ethics and Order Complex: A Sociological Interpretation to Chinese Thought*. Taipei Huge Stream Press, 1995.)

Buddhism.

The Buddhist faith came to China from India. The scriptures were brought from India to China by Chinese monks, who translated them into Chinese. The religion quickly caught on with the massses. It adapted itself to Chinese culture and ways. And for several hundred years over-shadowed Confucianism in the court and with the common people. During China's Golden Age of the Tang dynasty (618-907) the Chan form of Buddhism was taken to Japan and is known today as Zen Buddhism.

Other religions including Christianity have entered China many times, the first being during Europe's Dark Ages. Islam came to China via the Silk Route by traders from Syria and Arabia in the seventh century. In modern times Christian missions to China began in the early 19th century.

In China today Christians are trying a new approach they call 'post-denominational' churches. This is an effort to develop in the Chinese churches the best of Protestant denominations with as few of the Western denominational mistakes and detours as possible. It is an important step in the development of a Chinese Christian theology. It is an attempt worth putting on our prayer calendars. (For more on the churches of China and the post denominational phenomenon see my book, *Christianity in Today's China*, published by <1stBooks.com>. The book can be downloaded from the

Internet or purchased in bookstores.)

Among the many who made this book possible, special appreciation is due Kent Keith, director of The Texas Collection, Baylor University and the archivist Ellen Brown. I am indebted to many who read early drafts and made priceless suggestions; mistakes in grammar or typos are mine.

Britt Towery
July 28, 2000

A Glossary of Terms

There have been many systems of writing the sounds of Chinese words into Roman letters. The present system is called pinyin and is used by the United Nations and all over mainland China. The spelling of Chinese words in Roman alphabet used by Carey and Jewell are in parentheses.

Beijing	(Peking, sometimes Peiping or P'ei P'ing)
Dao	(Tao, the religion)
Dengzhou	(Teng Chow, now Pingdu)
Guangzhou	(Kuangtung or Canton)
Henan	(Honan Fu, a province bordering Shandong)
Huangdi	(Huang Ti, the yellow emperor)
Huangxian	(Huanghsien or Huanhien)
Jinan	(Tsi Nan)
Kong Fuzi	(K'ung Fu Tzu or Confucius)
Laiyang	(Lai Yang)
Laizhou	(Lai Chow or Lai Chou)
Penglai	(Teng Chow)
Pingdu	(Pingtu or Ping Tu in the Daniel's day)
Qingdao	(Ch'ing T'ao City or Ching Tao)
Qing dynasty	(Ch'ing or Ching dynasty)
Shandong	(Shantung or Shan Tung)
Suzhou	(Soo Chou or Soochow)
Tianjin	(Tientsin, port city for Beijing)
Yangzi	(Yangtze Kiang, longest river in China)
Zhifu	(Chefoo, Chee Foo or Che Fu, the area of the city of Yan'tai where many of the missionaries and other foreigners lived.)

11

1
SHANDONG SUMMER STORM

A saddled, riderless horse was not a common sight on the Shandong plains of China. As some venturesome peasants attempted to catch the horse, it ran from them. It did not stop until outside the city of Laiyang. There it waited in the rain and cold of the night until the city gates were opened.

At first light, villagers walked upstream to see what took place during the mountain storm of the previous night. Rivers and streams of Shandong are famous for flash floods. Water could come down from the hills and the gullies, flooding the usually dry river bed. In minutes the parched earth became a vast expanse of rushing water. There was never any warning to travelers, fishermen or boat people. A day could be bright and clear, but a storm in the mountains could turn a barely visible stream into a flooding torrent in minutes.

The peasants knew the horse belonged to a foreigner. For one thing the saddle was too expensive for a peasant Chinese. One of the men called out to *bai ma* — Old White, the foreigner's horse, but to no avail. Besides, very few dirt farmers in that part of China could even afford a riding horse. Few even had mules or oxen to plow their fields.

As the horse galloped homeward one or two of the villagers recognized the horse. It belonged to the sandy-haired foreigner who had been riding from village to village for over a year telling of his foreign religion. Carey Daniel was at home on a horse, having grown up in Texas. He was more used to larger horses but he liked Old White, as he called his Mongolian pony. His clean-cut features and ever-ready smile made him a favorite wherever he stopped to share his faith. He believed in making friends before trying to introduce his faith. This was a slower approach, but he felt it was the best approach. The Chinese among whom he worked had a history and society centuries older than his own back home in America.

When the crops were in and the farmers had time, they listened, many out of curiosity, to his funny-sounding

13

Chinese. They never ceased to wonder why such a pale-skinned man from another world kept wandering through their villages. While many were merely curious, others listened intently, looking for something that made sense to them; something they might find spiritually fulfilling — even if it was from a different looking man. He was well-liked, and when he spoke Chinese it had the flavor of the local *Shandong hua* — Shandong dialect. That was one reason they remembered him — the strange-looking fellow who spoke almost like they did and not like the Standard Mandarin speakers from the capital in Peking. That and his smile that seemed to always be on his sun-burned face.

It was Sunday, June 28, 1914. It was hot in the western reaches of the Shandong peninsula. The four-year missionary, fast becoming a veteran, was anxious to get home to his wife. She was expecting their first child. The stream had been no problem to cross on his way out to preach in the villages. The slowing rising stream could be crossed, he thought, but none of the locals were willing to ferry him across. He and Old White could swim that river and get back to his wife, waiting in Laiyang.

Carey Daniel had been married four months. Jewell Legett, his lovely bride, now pregnant, did not go with him on this preaching tour. It was his first time to be away from his bride, and he was anxious to see her. Heavy rains had turned the mountain streams into flooding torrents. Ordinarily these are not dangerous. This day, in the Jao Gia Dwang village, west of their home in Laiyang, Carey had preached to a handful of believers and inquirers, baptizing some new converts and helping with church business meetings. Laiyang County had over a million people, most of them never having heard of the Jesus about whom Carey preached.

Carey told her how much he was looking forward to returning after this trip because in the past he never had a wife to come home to. He was always greeted by Chinese men, his cook or the gatekeepers. Now he had her to return to.

Carey learned to ride horses and donkeys as a boy. At one time, while at Baylor University and working in Hill County as a missionary, he had a horse and buggy. But for him astride a horse was the only way to travel. In China wagons were rare, wheelbarrows too slow and uncomfortable, and young men did not ride in *shentzes* (A basket-like conveyance carried on two poles by four men, sometimes by a mule or two). He also trusted Old White and felt secure in making the plunge across the river without waiting. Carey thought he could reach home by eight but Jewell waited the whole night long, hoping something had prevented his starting home. She knew he was eager to get home and was a man of his word.

One of the peasants said he knew who the missing horseman was, for late Sunday he had advised a foreigner to wait until the river subsided before trying to cross. That usually took several hours and the foreigner was too eager to get home to his new bride. Impatience was a trait in foreigners that the Chinese could never fathom. Why did everything have to be done in such a hurry, they thought.

At White Dragon River he asked some villagers to ferry him across but they refused and he and Old White headed out to swim the swollen river.

About six o'clock on Monday morning as Jewell was dressing, she heard the gatekeeper cry in a most alarmed voice, "*Can ju, can ju* — O terrible, terrible, Mrs. Daniel!" She ran to the gate and there the most dejected and tired looking animal she ever saw stood shaking in the morning air. It was Old White, hair wet and clinging, saddle soaked, bridle gone. Almost beside herself, wishing the horse could speak, her mind and heart went out in all directions. He had carried Carey tens of thousands of miles and now could not tell her what had happened!

She sent the gatekeeper post-haste for Mr. Wang their personal language teacher and dear friend. She led the sad frame of a Mongolian pony back to the feed house and fed him. When Old White was rested she intended to have Mr. Wang ride him back along the road to Jao Gia Dswang and find out what had happened. If only Old White could have entered the city last night and they could have begun earlier to search for Carey. Carey had told her of his having often reached the gates after night fall to find them closed. All cities had suburbs and inns outside the city walls. She hoped for anything. May be he was ill in one of the inns and they would find him.

Mr. Wang came immediately, like the kindly Christian gentleman he was, bringing with him Old Wei, the carpenter. On their way to the West gate they stopped at the house of the only two Christian women in the city and sent one of them to Jewell. They had already told the gatekeeper that he must not leave *Dan si-niang* (Sister Daniel) under any circumstances whatever.

As Wang and Wei retraced Carey's steps some villagers told them that they heard him singing as he rode through the heavy rain the night before. Carey was know for his singing on such trips.

Monday wore away, a hideous nightmare for Jewell. Along in the afternoon the head teacher at the boy's school, Mr. Ga Dze-tao, insisted she send telegrams to the other mission stations. Missionary colleagues Anna Pruitt and Tully Foster McCrea immediately set out from Chefoo for Laiyang to be with Jewell. William Carey Newton and Wiley B. Glass set out on horseback from Huangxian to help Edgar L. Morgan, of Laizhou City, search for Carey. During those endless days, before any foreigners could reach Jewell, the Chinese at Laiyang did all anyone could do. They came and sat with her and prayed with and for her. By Wednesday Jewell could restrain herself no longer. She had to go to the river and join in the search. "I wish I could make you realize," she wrote to friends a year later, "how kind the people were. As I passed down the streets, the old heathen men would inquire with trembling voices, '*Dan si niang*, have you found any trace of his body yet?'"

The women of the town, both Christian and non-believers, spoke to her so tenderly that she knew "they wanted to get their hands on me to 'love me.'"

On the fourth day of the search the missionaries and Chinese villagers stumbled along the sandbar without hope of finding him. Then they were frozen by what they saw a few feet away. A greyish-white human hand reaching up out of the sand. It appeared to be groping for a rope or hand to pull it from the smothering muck of wet sand. They had found the body of *Dan mushi* (Pastor Daniel).

Straw mats were brought out to cover the body once it was dug out of the sand. There had been no deterioration of the body. The cold wet sand had perserved the handsome Texan but exposure to the hot summer air quickly changed all that. Jewell was not allowed to see the body. He was lifted from the river bed and placed in a local coffin in the courtyard of a Chinese temple outside the west gate of the city of Laiyang.

The young widow stood bravely before the Chinese coffin. She had stood before coffins before but never with such heartbreak as this. Death in this famine and flood stricken area of Shandong had become all too common place. Jewell Legett Daniel "lived years in those four awful days," wrote Edgar Morgan in the September, 1914, issue of *The Foreign Mission Journal*. He went on to write, "A great volume of prayer went up for her and for all the relatives at home. Those who saw her in the trial testify to the wonderful triumph she had over death and all its fears. She is a most remarkable woman, and is so brave."

She was told the body would rest there until cold weather when it could be taken to the foreign cemetery in Chefoo. The funeral service was held in the courtyard of their home and Jewell, numb and confused, prepared to return to America.

The annual conference of the North China Baptist Mission was to begin Monday night, July 6, 1914. Effort began immediately to get Jewell to Shanghai where she could board a ship for the States. Even before this she hated the sea. She could become sea sick just looking at the water. Now she must not only return broken-hearted across the world's largest ocean alone but expecting Carey's child. But for the moment such thoughts were farthest from her mind.

She stood silently in the temple where Carey's body lay and prayed and prayed. What could be the meaning of such a sudden tragic end to their lives, to their ministry? It seemed their years in Texas as students at Baylor University and later in Louisville, Kentucky, were now only a dream. Was all that went before real? Was all this some cruel joke? Is all this really happening? It was evident to them that their city of Laiyang was just beginning to show signs of opening to the Gospel message in an unusual way. The people had come to love Carey for he had the gift of friend-making. The others left her alone there at the temple with her love. She tried to reconcile the sudden, drastic change that seemed to wipe out her life. What had been such a happy beginning to ministry was crushed. Her lifelong call to China, a call she had felt from God since childhood — is this all there is? — can it end like this? Had she come to *Shenzhou* (an ancient name for China, meaning, "God's Country.") merely to be humiliated and crushed? — had life ended before was it even began? She would ponder the questions overland to Cheefoo and on a steamer to Shanghai where she caught an ocean-going vessel for America.

2
The Girl from Buffalo Gap

Jewell Legett was born August 15, 1884 in Buffalo Gap, a village fifteen miles south of Abilene, Texas. The families of both her parents migrated to Buffalo Gap in 1880. Her father, Tom Riley Legett, known to his friends as T. R., came with his parents (Judge Kernie K. Legett, later chairman of the trustees of Simmons College [Hardin Simmons University], Abilene, Texas, and Mintie Berry Legett) from Monticello, Arkansas. Alice came to Buffalo Gap with her parents, Alice and William Herring, from Llano, Texas.

Buffalo Gap was something of a gate, a natural passage-way through which buffalo and the original Americans (long before they were called Indians) had traveled for centuries. Closer to Legett's own time the Anglo cattlemen called it the Dodge Cattle Trail as they took their beef cattle from Texas to market in Kansas. The well-preserved Buffalo Gap historical village is about all that remains today, but it gives a good imitation of what life was like a hundred years ago for a farm girl born on the Texas frontier.

It did not take long for T. R. Legett and Alice Herring to fall in love. On September 11, 1881, a year after their families settled in Texas, T.R. and Alice were married in Llano County. T. R. was almost 27 and Alice was two weeks from her seventeenth birthday. T. R. soon opened a drugstore in Abilene and became known as a "horseback preacher." He went to places often neglected or without regular church services. He was also for a time, pastor of the Buffalo Gap Baptist Church.

Jewell was their first child. Growing up in a devout Bible-reading and Bible-believing home it was natural for her to feel the call of God to missionary work. She made no bones about it in later years that God had clearly called her — in her childhood — to missionary life in China. She was human enough to have doubts and to even dread thinking of what existence would be like in China. For five years, from the moment of her call to China, she told no one of the matter.

She lived a lonely life trying to decide whether missionary work, and in China of all places, was the real thing God wanted her to do.

She got fresh encouragement for her life's work when she learned that the day she was born her father lifted her in his arms to God and "gave me to Him" for missionary service. Her father was pastor of the First Baptist Church of Buffalo Gap, and his act of dedication of her to God was the most normal thing he knew to do. She grew up under the piety of a preacher's home on the Texas frontier.

Jewell's family moved to Sherwood and Arcadia before finally settling in 1896 on the Texas Gulf Coast town of Port Lavaca. The Legetts bought a home on North Street and opened a drugstore on Main Street. T. R. Legett often supplied the pulpit of the First Baptist Church of Port Lavaca and preached in many outlying areas. A place that cried out for his help was in the Swedish community of Olivia. He was able to secure the use of the school building and begin a Sunday School. Most of the Swedes were Lutherans, but cooperation between denominations was more common in those days, and his Baptist approach was welcome in the community. Once a month he would take the boat from Port Lavaca to Olivia on a Saturday, spend the night with church members, and hold services on Sunday. He would spend Sunday night with another family and return on the Monday morning boat to his Port Lavaca drugstore.

Jewell's mother, Alice, was a nurse and a great help in T. R.'s pharmaceutical work. With her husband's help Alice dispensed medicines to those in need. During the Flu Epidemic of 1917-1918 they both contracted the flu. Alice was not able to shake off the effects of the flu and died of pneumonia February 13, 1917. She was 53. T. R. recovered from the flu but never fully recovered from the loss of Alice. He died July 12, 1922, almost 68 years of age. Both of Jewell's parents, dedicated to their Lord and their community, died long before their time.

Jewell's conversion experience came when she was 13, the year after the family moved to Port Lavaca. She was baptized by Rev. A. Marsh during the summer of 1897.

Jewell entered Baylor University the first time in 1902. Hardly two months into her studies she took ill with typhoid fever. She was put in a "sick room" on the campus, where no visitors were allowed, with no books or papers, only quiet time alone with her God. When she was able to travel, she returned to Port Lavaca to recuperate under the loving care of her nurse-mother. After a year at home, with her strength and health restored, she returned to Baylor where she immediately became involved in activities of the Foreign Mission Band. The Foreign Mission Band was organized on the second floor of Old Main in 1900 by missionary-minded men like W. B. Glass, H. H. Muirhead and J. Frank Norris.[1]

The Baylor Foreign Mission Band was an outgrowth of the work of Professor John S. Tanner's Worker's Band, which was somewhat inspired by the spirit of Charles M. Sheldon's book, *In His Steps*. The Worker's Band's motto came from the question ask throughout Sheldon's book, on all occasions, "What would Jesus do?"

The actual formation of the Baylor Foreign Mission Band was a result of the November, 1900, campus revival. A. W. McGaha, pastor of the Waco First Baptist Church, brought the messages in the chapel of Carroll Library. Nothing much happened until B. L. Lockett announced in a prayer meeting that God was calling him to Africa. The prayer meetings got more serious. Harvy Harold Muirhead[2] surrendered to go to Brazil and J. M. Benson was called to Mexico. After praying far into the night the men retired, but the revival had begun.

In the services the following day, W. B. Glass told the group he had already decided to go to China but affairs at home needed his attention before he could go.

From such beginnings, the Baylor Foreign Mission Band emerged. Members met once a week, led services in the jails, city hall and mission points. They wrote to missionaries, requesting first-hand reports on their work. Lottie Moon was one of the earliest to respond to the volunteer mission band. She wrote July 21, 1903 from her home in Pingdu, China. Baylor graduates as they went to the mission fields corresponded with the group for years to come. From 1900 to 1916, including Jewell and Carey, more than 15 former Baylor

Band members wrote back to encourage the group.[3]

Professor John S. Tanner (1869-1901), a unique and influential teacher at Baylor was the driving force in beginning the band. Future missionaries — like W. B. Glass, and Muirhead and future renouned Southern Baptist theologian W. T. Conner — were inspired by John Tanner's example, spirit and intellect. Tanner taught philosophy, psychology, and mathematics but delighted in teaching the English Bible. W. B. Glass, who lived in Tanner's home his sophomore year at Baylor and later went to China as a missionary, said of him, "His chapel talks were exceedingly inspiring and often filled with visions of the world's millions for whom Christ died and were still waiting for the first news of his redeeming grace."

From Baylor Jewell wrote her parents about her decision to answer God's call to foreign missions. Her father told her, "Girly, when you were born, I took you from your mother's side. I lifted you up in my hands and gave you to God to be a foreign missionary." Her parents had never told her this until now. Nor had she hinted before of being called of God in her teens. Her father told her, "I wanted you to be God-called, not Dad-called."[4]

The minutes of the volunteer band meeting of April 9, 1906, recorded Jewell's report on the Student Volunteer Movement Conference held in Nashville, Tennessee, February 27 to March 2, 1906. She had been elected by the group to attend. Her report was mostly on a message by John R. Mott on the price of leadership. She called it "The Pastor as a Spiritual Force in the World's Evangelization."

Jewell and Carey graduated in 1907. She and Carey Daniel were fortunate to be at Baylor those early years of the 20th century. In addition to the visionary president, S. P. Brooks, the school had one of the finest faculties in America at the time.

Heading the list were men like Alfred Henry Newman, professor of Church History and writer of history textbooks used for more than fifty years in colleges and universities; Calvin Goodspeed, professor of Systematic Theology and New Testament translator; Charles B. Williams, professor of biblical Greek and Theology, translated the most readable and accurate English translations of the New Testament (which is still in print); Henry Lee Hargrove, professor of English language and literature, had a heart for missions and taught English in China for over a dozen years. (Hargrove's daughter, Auroria Koons Morrow, returned to China as a missionary in the 1920s). John Kern Strecker was Assistant Librarian and Curator of the Baylor Museum; Francis G. Guittard was assistant professor history and political science. Dorothy Scarborough was an assistant lecturer in English.

Jewell's dorm mother, wife of professor A. H. Newman, was considered "a tender heart but with a will inflexible" by the women students she supervised in Burleson Hall.

B. H. Carroll, dean of the College of Theology (which later became Southwestern Baptist Theological Seminary in Fort Worth, Texas) was also president of the University Board of Trustees. Pat M. Neff, was vice president of the trustees and later Governor of Texas and president of Baylor University. Other trustees of note were George W. Truett of Dallas and Jeff D. Ray.

Among Jewell and Carey's classmates was a future missionary to Brazil, Taylor Crawford Bagby. Bagby sang second tenor in the Glee Club and wrote his graduating thesis on a subject influenced by his growing up in Catholic Brazil, "Clericalism: Behold the Enemy!"

Thomas Hendricks Taylor of May, Texas, was in graduate studies in 1907. He was an honor graduate of Howard Payne College (then a two-year institution). Tom Taylor later became a long-time legend of a president of Howard Payne College. A quote beside his name in the 1907 Baylor annual, *The Round-Up*, read: "Men are not always what they seem, first appearances deceive many." Such was true of this man whose favorite (or often used) speech in years to come was "Every tub stands on its own bottom." Taylor's graduating thesis was "Why the Solid South?"

Conway King played first horn in the Baylor Band. Later King was associated with the great marching band leader of the century and composer, John Philip Sousa. King was versatile on every instrument and led many of his high school bands to high honors in Texas, including having his 1947 Brownwood High School band voted the best band in Texas at the San Antonio Battle of Flowers.

One other classmate should be noted here. He was a ministerial student from Mt. Vernon, Illinois, named John Quintin Herrin. He came to Baylor in 1902 and the next year was the winner of the Scholarship Contest. He was president of the Student's Christian Association. He wrote his thesis on "Commission government of our municipalities." Some thirteen years after Carey Daniel's death Jewell married John Herrin.

After graduation from Baylor, in the fall of 1907, Jewell taught school in Goodnight, Texas. The temptations that had come to her at Baylor to ignore the call to China came to her again as she began teaching. Influences as silent as the memories of her friends and teachers at Baylor were strong when they needed to be. Through prayer she overcame her excuses to stay out of missions, and entered the Woman's Missionary Union Training School in Louisville, Kentucky. (This school was recently closed by the ultra-conservative leaders of the Southern Baptist Convention, despite its having been the leading missionary training facility for Baptists of the South for nearly a century.) It was here she said she wanted "to get ready for my life in China." The one year in the "home-school" did wonders for her spirit and calling to missions.

At the Louisville school she learned much more about prayer; how important Christian fellowship can be; recognized more clearly the beautiful things of life; but most of all she learned to be willing, even glad, to take up her calling with new enthusiam. Jewell got a new vision of a lost world and especially the need in China.

3
THE COWBOY PREACHER

Joseph Carey Daniel was the son and grandson of Baptist preachers. His father, George Mayfield (G.M.) Daniel (1846-1918), was born in Floyd County, Georgia, on January 27, 1846. G.M. married Sarah Elizabeth Virginia Lowery (1849-1931) January 20, 1870. Together they raised six sons and four daughters. G.M. was baptized at 14 by Elder Hugh Carmichael in the Chatahoochee River. He served with Company E, 17th Alabama Regiment of the Confederate Army. G. M. Daniel came to Texas in 1867 and was ordained to the ministry in November 1873. It was said that "no tongue knows how to say ill of him." Carey wrote in his 1907 book, *History of Hill County Baptists,* that his father organized 12 churches and baptized more than 1200 people. Most of that work was done when he served as moderator of the Evergreen Association in southeast Texas. In 1905 the Daniel family moved to Tyler, Texas, where Carey's father served as the Baptist missionary of the Smith County Association.

War deprived Carey's father of the education he desired. Because of this lack of formal training, he saw to it that each of his children received a college education. Joseph Carey Daniel was the fifth child of the G. M. Sarah's children. The seventh child was Marion Price Daniel, father of Price Daniel, a U.S. senator and governor of Texas, and William P. Daniel, governor of Guam. These two men, and others, of the Daniel line carried on the spirit of their China missionary uncle, a spirit that would never give up, regardless of the odds. So Carey was an uncle to future governors. The Daniel men, taking after G. M. Daniel, the Alabama preacher and Confederate soldier — who never let anything discourage him — never felt any task too small or too great to challenge and overcome.

In correspondence and his writings Carey Daniel signed himself "J.C. Daniel." But to his friends and family he was always "Carey." His home, until he entered college in 1902, was in Willis, Texas, a town much like the Governor Bill and

Vara Daniel Historic Village.[5] Carey Daniel pastored the Center Church, east of Mt. Calm, and the Mesquite Church five miles northeast of Mt. Calm. In 1904 Carey was present for the organization of the Calvary Baptist Church in the town of Whitney. On September 7, 1905, he helped organize the Parr's Chapel Church which was five miles east of Hillsboro. The same year he organized and pastored the Malone Church. The Malone Church made history the following year, 1906, when it was host for the occasion of the consolidation of the Hill County Baptist Association and the Hillsboro Baptist Association. The Baptists and their churches of Hill County were learning to work together.

The year Carey graduated from Baylor, 1907, he published a book on Baptist work in the Hillsboro, Texas, area entitled, *A History of the Baptists of Hill County, Texas.* He "sunk some money" into the project and evidently did not make much, if any, profit from this early venture into the literary world.[6] Had there been more books like this, the saga of Texas Baptists would be more than just the minutes of churches and reports of conventions. Carey dedicated his book as follows:

> To Elder G. M. Daniel, my father in the flesh
> and to Elder M. A. Cornelius, my father in the ministry,
> who are representative of the great host of
> faithful associational missionaries in Texas,
> this volume is affectionately dedicated.

Pastor M. A. Cornelius, whom Carey notes as his father in the ministry, was born July 7, 1846, in Cherokee County, Alabama. The elder Cornelius spent four years in the Alabama legislature and two years as a member of Confederate General Wheeler's Cavalry during the Civil War. At the time Carey dedicated this book to him and G. M. Daniel, Cornelius was the associational missionary for Hill County. Cornelius' son, E.S. Cornelius, was one of Carey's closest friends at Baylor and later at Southern Seminary.

In his book on Hill County Baptists, Carey records the names of pastors and churches going back to J. M. Sanford who was thought to be the first Baptist preacher to live in Hill County. Sanford settled in 1847 halfway between Itasca and Milford. Carey wrote what one of Sanford's contemporaries said about preacher Sanford: "He was brave, brave as a lion, whether facing the savage Indian or fighting Satan for the souls of men."

Preachers were as a rule poor men, few had a finished education. "However," as Carey writes, "they loved their Bibles and loved lost souls. All the week they toiled to support their families and would ride many miles to their monthly appointment on Saturday and Sunday. Their presence cheered the Christians, inspired the children and drew respect from the heart of the hardened sinner."

Most of the country churches had "preaching" only once a month or every other Sunday, as preachers were few. The Methodists were not the only circuit riders in those days. A Baptist pastor might farm all week and every weekend go to a different church to preach and minister to the community. On other Sundays, when there was no preacher, the churches would have "singings" and Sunday Schools, led by laymen.

One pioneer to Hill County was J. H. Dyer. He was Hill County's first judge and he and his wife were converted there in 1855. In Carey's Hill County Baptist history, he wrote: "At the close of the Civil war Dyer led a colony to South America rather than yield to the Union flag and republican oppression." Dyer's wife died there, and in 1872 he and his two sons returned to Texas.

In the last part of the book Carey gives a summary chapter on the early Baptists of England and the development of the American Baptist experience. Baptists going overseas as missionaries were sent out from Boston. After more than twenty years of cooperation the Boston board informed their Southern brethren they would cease sending slave-owning missionaries in the future. The Baptist leaders of the South did not take kindly to this and broke from their Northern brethren. In May, 1845, the Southern Baptist Convention was organized.

Without giving his sources, Carey states that in 1845 there were 250,000 white Baptists in the South and 100,000 Negroes. He states that in 1907 there were 1,899,427 white

Baptists and 1,941,653 black Baptists. For many years the black Baptists had their own conventions. S. E. Brooks of Alabama settled in Hill County in 1868 and is credited with beginning the Towash Baptist Church, the first black church in the area. S.E. Brooks was the father of S. P. Brooks, president of Baylor University when Carey was in school.

At the beginning of the 20th century, the Nord [North] Texas German Baptist Association reported: "There are over 300,000 Germans in Texas and every one has a soul to save." In Falls County alone there were eight German-language churches.[7]

The 1907 Baylor University annual, *The Round-Up*, Carey is listed among the "Who's Who in Baylor" as "the bravest" of the students. There is a full-page pen and ink sketch, a caricature, of Carey. It and the words below the picture make good fun that he has been at Baylor "for the last part of the last century ... he's very meek and refined, and pertickerly eloquent at prayer meetings." ("Pertickerly" is not misspelled here. That was a part of the humor of the cartoon and sentiment.)

Carey worked for the Texas Mission Board as State Evangelist during the last half of 1907, holding revival meetings in Aquilla, Whitney, Osceola, Prairie Valley, Groesbeck and Teague. It took more than one job to make ends meet. He also served as field secretary for Baylor University. That fall he attended the annual meeting of the Texas Baptist Convention in San Antonio. Attending such gatherings, Carey met some of the Texas Baptist pioneers. He often felt his own life and ministry was far short of theirs. He wrote in his diary:

> My life is very, very far from what it should be. I do not pray enough, do not read my Bible enough and do not live pure enough. I have the consolation that God knows how in my heart I long to do the right thing. God's grace helping me, I'll try to do better and more. God forgive me of my sins.

28

4
CAREY AT BAYLOR

Before going to Baylor, Carey hoed cotton, planted crops, taught school and worked at all sorts of jobs, like any other farm boy of the times. It was during these formative years he came to be close to Anthony Frank, later principal of the Conroe High School, whom he met in 1893. W. C. Hamil, editor of the *Baptist Echo*, was a friend.

Carey, whose father and grandfather were Baptist preachers, began to feel urgings to preach the summer of 1899. On November 5, 1899, he preached his first sermon to a congregation gathered under large trees in Union Grove Church, Texas. He preached at Willis, Middle Caney, Hickory Grove and Willow Creek in the weeks following. He was licensed to preach the Gospel November 26 and two weeks later married his first couple (Wiley Pitts and Lizzie Purvis). Five days before Christmas he preformed his second such ceremony (W. F. Freemon and Ellen Kelley).

The opening month of the twentieth century found him at home with his parents and brothers and sisters celebrating the Christmas season. He apparently had no difficulty meeting young ladies. His diaries mention Miss Vernon Long of Rush; Ella Margaret Davis; Lillie Darden ("a true friend to me" he wrote after her untimely death); Leona Gentry; Edna Blachshear and Beulah Roane. He met Edna and Beulah at at State Sunday School and Colportage Convention in San Antonio in 1896.

When not preaching he attended services at Waco's Third Street Baptist Church, Edgefield Baptist Church and later joined for a while the Seventh and James Baptist Church. His ordination to the ministry came over a year later, June 23, 1901.

His first pastorate was with the Mesquite Church in Hill County. Later he added to his duties the same work with the Friendship Church in Limestone County. In August of 1901 Carey held his first baptismal service at the Mt. Calm Baptist Church.

Once in Huntsville he was "fined costs and etc., about

$90 for having whipped Cleveland Davis at Gladstone." He fills in no details of this encounter but added, "It costs heavily sometimes to do your duty."

A classmate, J. Frank Norris, was often mentioned in Carey's diary. He relates the event of Norris' wedding to Miss Lillian Gaddy. Norris led the fight to purge Texas and Southern Baptists of the liberals and modernists, as he perceived them to be, in the 1920s and 1930s.

Haydenites (followers of Dr. S. A. Hayden) were a constant problem in Carey's ministry at the Center Church. Hayden pre-dated Norris in trying to purge the Texas Baptist Convention. Carey felt personally affronted because A. Lowery, his grandfather (his mother's father), was a charter member of the Texas Baptist Convention. Carey felt a loyalty to Texas Baptists through a heritage of blood and spirit.

At a Center Church Conference in 1902, it became necessary to exclude one preacher, its former pastor, and three others from membership in the church. Carey writes in his diary that the former pastor, another preacher and three others were "declared guilty of a grave charge. I regret to be entangled in a disturbance of such character, but believe it to be for God's glory." Those excluded and others that went with them formed the Bowman Missionary Baptist Church and filed suit for the Center Church property. Carey said the property was not worth the cost of a suit but does not record what happened.

At the Mertens Church a Mrs. M. E. Beaver was excluded from the fellowship of that church. He writes: "Quite a turmoil was had during conference in the midst of which I was slapped in the face by the good sister, and she made an effort to put me out of the house by force. It was exceedingly ugly and I regretted it very much. I love peace and desire to pursue it. God bless all people with whom I work and help me to love everybody." Nobody said being a Baptist was easy.

One November night he went out and spent time with Waco's revelers. He did it merely as "a matter of education." After supper he finished his work at the Baylor Chapel where he was serving as janitor and set out for town. First he visited a Pentecostal "Holy-Rollers" meeting and "saw them carry on loud shoutings, and some things arousing my sympathy, some arousing my pity, and others my information."

Next he walked over to the flower show where he enjoyed the beauty of the flowers and arrangements but the sterioptican show scenes were "half vulgar." Apparently he saved the worst for last. He went to a dance hall. Here he said "the art (?) of dancing was being taught. There were 17 young ladies dancing with as many young men." He was impressed by the "beautiful forms and graceful movements" but felt it was not a place for a young Baptist preacher. He summarized, in nineteenth century English, his educational night on the town as increasing his decided dislike for "the debased worship at shrines of worldliness" which are "fleeting delusive shadows of Satan" and "enough to bring blushes to the faces of beholding angels."

Oct 29, 1901, Carey saw his first football game between Baylor and University of Texas. In his diary he left this impression of the sport:

> This afternoon I paid fifty cents to see a game of football between the team of the State University and Baylor. It was my first sight of the kind, and I pronounce it as my candid, deliberate conviction that it is the most brutal, unnecessary and harmful thing I ever thought college bred people to tolerate. Many good and wise people admire the game and advocate its stay and growth. God speed the day when the extra energy and time of Baylor students may be given to something more ennobling, kind and God-like.

On November 1, 1906, Carey mentions witnessing another football game. The years may have mellowed him but not regarding the gridiron. The game was between the University of Arkansas and Baylor. Baylor won, 11-6. He wrote: "It is much like a bull fight, only they were human beings and not angry."

He closed his diary a year before his graduation from

Baylor, never once mentioning Jewell Legett. Although on Feb 5, 1906, he received a letter from his mother in which he comments, "she hears I'm married. It is not true, but I really wish I was in position to marry."

Carey met numerous dignitaries of the times. He once attended a speech by Texas Governor James Stephen Hogg at the Waco City Hall. He and his friend Anothy Frank heard the 25th president of the United States, William McKinley, speak twice in Austin. McKinley was assassinated in 1901. Carey's diary reveals he once "clasped the hand of President Theodore Roosevelt when he passed through Waco."

Carey wrote the song "Our Baylor" sung to the tune of *America*. He won the Baylor Annual 1907 *Round Up* prize for writing and singing it.

During the Spring of the year 1908, Carey Daniel held a number of revival meetings in Lexington and Giddings, Texas churches. On Sunday, March 8th, he closed a revival meeting at McGregor where fifty new members joined the church, 27 by baptism, 19 of these men and boys.

In August of 1908 Carey Daniel's 16-page pamphlet, "A Plea for Christian Education,"[8] was published by Order of the Education Commission of the Baptist institutions of higher education. In it he wrote "the best success of all our missions and benevolent enterprises depends in large measure on the success of our Christian schools."

Baylor (with 1351 students in 1907) was the only institution granting degrees. The other Baptist schools were still in the process or growing to that level. He wrote: "Our country's dangers are not so much in lack of intelligence as in lack of character. Christian school lays stress on character as well as intelligence." He urged pastors to share Christian education needs with the churches and thereby strengthen the Christian witness in all realms of life.

On October 1, 1908, Carey moved to Louisville, Kentucky, and began his studies at the Southern Baptist Theological Seminary. In his dorm room in New York Hall he was reunited with his Baylor roommate, E. S. Cornelius. It did not take him long to locate the other eight or nine students from Texas. He joined the Highland Baptist Church of

Louisville and admitted to himself that he could not see three days ahead financially but believed God would provide.

He got a welcome cable that Jewell Legett was arriving at the Illinois Central Station to begin her study at the Training School across the fields from the seminary. After teaching a year in West Texas, Jewell felt a greater peace regarding her call to mission work. She felt the need to attend the Training School in Louisville. Carey met her train and she went with him to a church where he was preaching that week.

Carey and Cornelius and another student, T.C. Bagby, son of Brazil missionary W. B. Bagby,[9] had dinner in the home of their pastor, L. W. Doolan. The occasion was to welcome to Kentucky these far-from-home Baylor graduates. This was especially true of Bagby who was the farthest from home in Brazil. That fall they came to know in a more personal way, professors such as J.M. Frost and such special visiting speakers on the campus as R. A. Torrey and J. T. Medcalf.

Meanwhile, across the way, the young women at the Training School — each with personal dreams and burdens regarding mission service — came to know each other and their various calls to mission service. Some made it clear they were unwilling to go to the mission field, while others had special family burdens that made going impossible. At the Training School the young women could share their hopes and dreams to others of like mind and spirit for the first time in their lives. It was not an easy time for a woman to strike out on her own, to be her own person. It was still very definitely "a man's world."

5
JEWELL'S LOUISVILLE PREPARATION

Jewell spent a lot of time in prayer when she was at Baylor and more at the Training School. She had to be sure that God's call to China was really for her. She searched the scriptures and joined with others in prayer about missions and ministry. Lettie Spainhour was one of those with her own special burden. Lettie wanted to go to Africa, but the Foreign Mission Board had a rule that they would not send single women to Africa. Lettie eventually worked this out in her heart and sailed with Jewell, Jane Lide and Miss Floy White to China.[10] Jewell found it difficult to find a quiet place for prayer on the Training School campus. Later, she would be a driving force in getting a special prayer room added to the facilities. It would be named after famed China missionary Lottie Moon and even have Lottie's desk. But that is getting ahead of Jewell's story. Her desire for a special place for the students to pray was not just the whim of an over-zealous missionary candidate. She wrote in her diary about the need for a prayer room and of her first mention of Southern Baptist's most famous missionary, Miss Lottie Moon:

> We agreed one day that we would pray together to our Father to enable us to do His will. And where could we pray? Bedrooms were full and running over, music rooms in use; dining-rooms and halls impossible; chapel too public. Every nook and cranny of that small first loved building was full of girls preparing for their life-work of serving Jesus. Then we thought of Miss Leachman's bit of a room and remembered that Miss Leachman, teacher, was out. We slipped into her room and kneeling in the tiny space between the bed and wall had our blessed day of prayer.

Other girls were praying about their life-work, too, and next morning Mrs. McLure, the principal, called Janie Lide and me into her room. The principal told us that week before she had received a letter begging for help for Miss Lottie Moon, at Tengchow [pinyin spelling: Dengzhou, now Penglai] in North China; and said, "The dear lady has clearly directed me to you two."

While entering her last term at the Training School, Jewell wrote Dr. R. J. Willingham, head of the Southern Baptist Foreign Mission Board in Richmond, Virginia. Her eight-line note said: "I have dedicated my life to God's service, and He has shown me plainly that He wants me to work in China. Will you please send me application blanks? We are praying for you and your work. Sincerely yours, (Miss) Jewell Legett. 334 E. Broadway, Louisville, Ky., Jan. 14, 1909."

At their missionary appointment service Jewell and "Janie" as everyone called Jane Lide, were hoping to be allowed to work with Miss Moon.[11] She writes about those days in May, 1909, and their appointment to mission work in China:

In May accordingly, we appeared before the Foreign Mission Board for examination, and so did Lettie and Floy White. Janie and I were asking to be sent to Tengchow, Lettie wanted to go to Africa, and Floy said nothing to us about her destination. I shall never forget that day. With old fashioned, delightful courtesy, Dr. R. J. Willingham, Secretary of the Foreign Mission Board; Dr. Samuel Porter and two other members of the FMB escorted us girls into the examination room and considerately and with sympathetic understanding, asked necessary questions.

Later the men candidates came in, and in that sacred room I stood beside Dr. Lockett,

Mr. Clark, and Mr. Davis — three who were with me in another sacred hour six years before when I joined the foreign mission band at Baylor University.[12] When we came out Dr. Willingham followed us girls and said, "Mrs. McLure's recommendation practically assured your appointment. Miss Spainhour, dear, as we are not sending single women to Africa, we have designated you for Soochow [Suzhou], China. Miss Lide will go to Miss Moon in Tengchow. Miss White," —with a broad smile— "to Mr. Adams, who is waiting for her in Tengchow." Then, laying his hand upon my arm, for he was afraid I would be disappointed, he said, "Jewell, we are sending you, not to Tengchow, but to Miss Moon's more beloved field, Pingtu [Pingdu]."

Jewell mentions that there was another man in the room the day she was appointed to China, giving only his name — J. Carey Daniel. She makes no other mention of him, possibly because he was told by the committee to wait a year and re-apply.

Carey followed the suggestion of the Foreign Mission Board committee and a year later he was appointed to work in the city of Huangxian in Shandong province. He learned his new home was to be in the city of Hwanghsien [Huangxian], not far from the port city of Longkou (Dragon's mouth). He was sent there because it was the direction the Shandong missionaries were beginning to expand. They had branched out from the churches of Crawford and Hartwell in Tengchow [now Penglai] westward. As it turned out, Huangxian was only four days travel south to Jewell's mission station in the city of Pingdu.

In the 1960s Jewell recalled her last night with her family before leaving for China. It was in 1909 in her parent's home in Port Lavaca, Texas:

The last night at home included family
prayers which we always had. Only this time
with a poignancy never before experienced.
Two young brothers, one seventeen and the
other twenty-two; papa, mamma and me.
Papa read the 23rd Psalm, then knelt and
prayed. When we arose from our knees
mamma sang in her clear, sweet soprano,
"There are angels hovering 'round." More
than fifty years ago that was, but it's as heavenly to me now as it was that night.

Jewell Legett was going on 25 the summer of 1909 when
she took the train at San Antonio, Texas, for the West Coast
and sailed as a Southern Baptist missionary to the North
China province of Shandong. She would learn much from
such Baptist pioneers as Lottie Moon, Martha Foster
Crawford[13] and C. W. Pruitt in Shandong peninsula villages
and towns once visited by the greatest of all Chinese sages,
Confucius.[14]

Though not as well known in Southern Baptist history as
Lottie Moon, C. W. Pruitt, a farm boy from Georgia, was one
of the most respected foreigners in China. He grew in spiritual stature among the Chinese almost from the time he
arrived in China, in 1881. Because of the urgent need in
China for preacher-missionaries among the Baptists, he left
the Southern Baptist Theological Seminary in Louisville,
Kentucky, and sought appointment to North China. Pruitt
loved the language, and with the aid of his language helper,
translated into Chinese, among other books and articles, the
classic *Commentary on Matthew* by his beloved seminary
teacher, John A. Broaddus. C. W. Pruitt would become one of
those they could count on in their brief missionary careers.

6
JEWELL AND
"FORM FITTING DRESSES"

Jewell was a lively young thing (she was tall for the times at five feet seven inches). Her blue eyes seemed always to be smiling and her burnet hair always shining. She joked in her diary about being more like a stick than a full-blown woman. She was far more than a stick in appearance. When she entered a room, people took notice. She was thrilled to be going to China with her classmate, Miss Floy White. On the train to the West Coast, Jewell saw a broad gold band on Floy's finger and "from the mischievous sparkle in her eyes" she decided to have some fun with Floy's ring.

It seems Floy had kept her engagement to Wayne Womack Adams secret the whole year of their study at Louisville from Jane Lide and Jewell. Once again Jewell's own words tell a lot about her and her times:

> I decided to have some fun with Floy. I totally ignored the ring. Didn't see it. All day we rode through broad Texas stretches, but there wasn't one word spoken about the ring, nor any wedding, nor any heart-sick swain. And at night Miss Floy grew sick of *ignorance* ! "Why don't you say something about my ring?" Hilarious laughter from both entirely broke the ice. "Don't you want to see his picture?" She inquired with dancing eyes, and I said, "Dying to!" And added at first glance, "Floy White, I wouldn't marry that man if he were the last one on earth! Look at that stubborn jaw!" But he was as good looking as they come and she was keenly happy at the prospect of the wedding due to take place in Miss Moon's home on our arrival in China.

Jewell and Floy, along with Lettie and Jane, "The Louisville Four," sailed from San Francisco on a ship she called "the hoary Old Middle Kingdom." The girls had a good introduction to China along the way, as missionary nurse Jessie Pettigrew was returning to China after furlough.[15] Jewell remembered the trip and her first meeting with Floy White's "Mr. Adams":

> Mr. Adams, Floy's beau-lover, was to meet us in Japan—and he didn't—not when we expected him to. Another bride-to-be was with us, a girl going out to marry a businessman in Japan. Her beau-lover (we never learned how he managed it) got her off ship in the darkness the first few hours we lay at anchor. But Mr. Adams didn't appear, and didn't appear. Morning came, morning passed, with never a word from him. Floy, sick with apprehension, remained in her cabin, while Jane, Lettie and I paced the deck watching for him. After what seemed days, I went below to have a word with Floy and came out of her room to go on deck again. And there at the top of the stairs was the tallest man I most ever saw, dressed in faultless black, with the very jaw on him I'd seen in the picture. In his arms were many of Japan's handsomest chrysanthemums and on his face an embarrassed and radiant smile. "My soul!" I cried and dashed for Floy's room, and I didn't beat him to it by many steps, I tell you. He came down those stairs six at a time, it seemed to me, and was right at my heels as I gasped, "Floy, he's come!" He dashed in as I dashed out and we continued our voyage in much peace and contentment.

Floy White was born in Brooklyn, Alabama, July 14, 1883. She graduated from Judson College in 1903 and the WMU Training School in 1907. The "Mr. Adams" who met her ship in Japan and married her in China a month later was Wayne W. Adams, a native of Pittsylvania County, Virginia. He had gone to China in 1908 doing mission work across the Bo Hai Sea from Shandong province in the Japanese-controlled port city now called Dalian.[16]

From Japan they sailed to Shanghai. There Lettie Spainhour left them to go inland to the city of Suchow [Suzhou], a part of the Central China Baptist Mission on the Yangzi River. The rest of the missionaries sailed on for the North China Baptist Mission on the Shandong peninsula. They traveled on a little Japanese steamer, "with an all-Japanese crew — thereby hangs a tale a mile long if there were only time to tell it, which there isn't." Jewell went on in her dairy without a clue to what "mile-long tale" she had in mind. She did come into rainy weather going up the China coast to the Shandong port of Yantai, then called Chefoo after the island-peninsula just off from the docks:

> There was only one first-class cabin and Floy, being the bride-to-be, got that. Jane and Mr. Adams and I were below decks, and sick, O ye little fishes! Will Jane and I ever forget that rough voyage from Kobe to Chefoo! When we arrived in the Chefoo harbor we lay at anchor four days while a terrible storm lashed the sea and our little vessel. We dared not try to land. We were finally taken off in Chinese sampans and deposited on a wind-swept dock. Only one human being had braved the storm to meet us. That was Miss Ida Taylor.[17] Miss Lottie Moon and the Dengzhou Baptist Station had sent her to escort Floy to the interior.
>
> A day or so in the Missionary Home in Chefoo and homes of missionaries and we were off again. Floy and Miss Taylor and Mr.

Adams to Dengzhou where Floy was to be Miss Moon's guest until the wedding one week later. I went to stay with the Ayers and Jessie Pettigrew in Hwang Hsien [Huangxian], 20 miles or half a day's journey from Dengzhou, until the wedding day. Floy and group went by shen-tze (mule litter) and we went by Peking cart.

Jewell was in her element in Huangxian. She had, in her own words, "a glorious" time. To see the mission work at first hand was an inspiration to this new recruit. She was excited to begin learning Chinese words, and she closely observed the customs and ways of the people — the people she said were from now on to be her people. She was thrilled to meet W.T. and Minnie Ayres and their family. Medical doctor W. T. Ayres began the first foreign mission hospital-clinic the Southern Baptists had overseas.[18] Jewell's first big undertaking was her friend's wedding. Here is how she recalled that day and the unexpected things Lottie Moon taught her:

October 28, 1909, the day of the wedding, finally arrived. Early were we on our way, in carts and mule-litters, to Dengzhou, a gay party indeed; added to the great joy of getting three new missionaries was not North China to have that rarest of all occurrences, a "foreigner's" wedding. When we arrived at Dengzhou we scattered out to various homes — Presbyterian ones, for the Baptists ones couldn't hold all of us. And besides, the Presbyterians were as excited over all the stir-up as the Baptists were!

After lunch we converged on the center of interest—Floy White. In true Chinese style, Floy had not gone to see her new home—and if Miss Moon had her way, and she probably did, Floy hadn't even seen the bride groom since he landed. Chinese brides didn't see grooms in that China until after the wedding ceremony, and Miss Moon was a great stickler for Chinese custom.

Jane and I were to be bridesmaids and the wedding was to be at 4:30. We helped with the preparations at the new home until the last minute then dashed into Miss Moon's house to dress. If we'd entered sedately and with studied grace, as Chinese young women, would have done it, would have gone much better. In our room a wail broke from the depths of me, for as we laid out our Training School Commencement dresses to put them on, I found a four inch cut in mine in a not inconspicuous place! A fold of it caught between the suitcase lid and rubbed through on the overland trip from Huangxian. This was truly one of the darkest moments of my life! But there was no time to grieve, no time to mend, and no other dress to wear. We had not only to dress quickly, but to compose ourselves enough to practice once more the little Training School blessing we were to sing at the end of the ceremony.

We heard Floy leave the house and knew that she was taking her place in the beautiful new sedan chair — gift of the groom — ready to be carried by coolies to her wedding. We hurried out too, only to be met by Miss Moon, face-to-face! I mean face-to-face, and her face was aghast. I know that is not good English, but no other words will convey any idea of Miss Moon's astonishment and great displeasure of our appearance.

"You are not going out of my house in those clothes!" She burst out at us. "Why, Miss Moon," we cried in dismay, "what's the matter with them? They're all we have!" Not until years later did we really understand what was the matter and sympathize with Miss Moon in her distress. Our dresses were form-fitting — very form-fitting. A Chinese woman's dress is made to conceal the lovely body-lines. To Miss Moon and to the hundreds of Chinese neighbors and friends gathered in the street, our dresses would be utterly indecent and vulgar. But the guests were gathered for the wedding, the bride was sitting demure in her chair — without Miss Moon's having seen her unrightness — and we just went right on as we were. But, many's the time since that I've wished we had done something — I can't think what — to save Miss Moon's feelings and our own good name in decent Chinese eyes.

Strange as it seems, that was my introduction to Lottie Moon, at least it was my first recollection of her. I had stayed in one of the Presbyterian homes the night before and Miss Moon, being the senior member of the Station and the hostess, was probably out of her home on a errand when I arrived. Maybe I met her on arrival, and she, just another of the many strangers, did not rise to the top of my dumb consciousness. Anyway, my first memory of her is the aforementioned one of incredulous face and horrified ejaculation.

Though Jewell admired and looked up to Miss Moon (not just figuratively, for Lottie Moon was nearly a good foot shorter than Jewell) she silently feared her. As did other missionaries. Not all, but some, found it best not to cross the old girl who came out to China in 1873. With the wedding of Floy and Wayne Adams over, and her introduction to China continuing, Jewell was anxious to get to her field of service in Pingdu and begin formal language study. She recalled her trip back to Huangxian and then her first trip to Pingdu this way:

The next morning, after the wedding feast, we went back to Huangxian for the night. The next day we set out for Pingdu. The long journey to the interior by shen-tze, that extremely uncomfortable method of "slow commotion" corn-popper, salt-shaker, cradle-motion, teeth-rattling, endurance test mode of conveyance was China's best at the time but torturing for a newcomer. I walked miles, until my limbs gave way, to keep from riding, but was most fortunate not to become shen-tze sick. We were a happy company on that long trip.

The first time I ever tried to get into a *shen-tze* strapped to mules was during this first month I was in China. We were coming with the Hearns from Dengzhou after Floy's wedding to Pingdu.[19] I was so new, green as a gourd. We were crossing the mountains between Laizhou and Pingdu and had been walking for a long while. I walked to keep from having to ride that miserable contraption. I kept wondering how in the world I was ever going to get into it. I found out pretty soon. Dr. Hearn had the driver stop the thing. He bent his knee and told me to hop up. I hesitated but knew I had to do it. So up I stepped, gave a spring and landed on my stomach across the *shen-tze* poll. I couldn't go on over for to do so would land me at the mule's heels. I couldn't go back for there was too much of me forwards. So there I balanced with Dr. Hearn holding my heels down. When I did finally wiggle in, I curled myself down in that old North China Pullman and spent

44

the afternoon meditating on the denizens of a people that causes them to go on century after century using such out-moded modes of travel. The night in the inn between Huangxian and Laizhou was an experience I've never forgotten tho' I spent many and many a night in Chinese inns in later years.

On the back of a picture of me in my new Chinese clothes I scribbled the following and sent it to Mr. Daniel in American before he sailed: "Mountains between Pingtu and Laichow. Notice the rocks in the foreground. North China mountains are almost solid rock streaked with seepage from many minerals. Janie said we had grown tired of being bumped and decided to Legett! Our front mule had a funny pi-ki—disposition. He insisted on lying down and rolling, two dozen times a day. You see his harness didn't prevent! During the day we passed a man on a bicycle. The bicycle frightened our mules. We girls got out to cover it with our skirts, and the skirts frightened them worse.

7
"LIFE IS LONG ENOUGH IF LIVED RIGHT"

Early in 1909 and before Jewell was appointed to China Carey had written to the Executive Secretary of the Foreign Mission Board, Rev. R. J. Willingham, about his willingness to go the mission field. At the time he was serving as pastor of the part-time Boston, Ky., Baptist Church. He would later take on another half-time church filling all his Sundays with preaching opportunities. Half-time churches had Sunday School lessons every Sunday but could only afford a preacher two Sundays a month. There were even quarter-time churches that had preaching only one Sunday a month. He preached in a nearby reformatory on occasion.

His interest in missions continued to grow. That Spring, W. B. Bagby spoke about his work in Brazil. With him was Miss Roxy Groves, who had a music degree from Howard Payne College and was attending Baylor University on a Howard Payne College scholarship. Roxy would later go to Brazil with the Bagbys and help in the church music programs. Roxy Groves, according to the 1907 Baylor annual, was the "most attractive" girl on the campus.

In all his writings, Carey spoke of Jewell as "Miss Jewell Legett." They and the other missionary recruits attended the 54th session of the Southern Baptist Convention in Louisville. Carey saw her and the other girls off at the Louisville train station when school was out in May. After her appointment to the mission field, Jewell spent the summer of 1909 with her parents before sailing for China.

Carey Daniel was not recommended by the Committee to be a missionary in 1909. He gave no reason but wrote simply they "...reported against sending me." He needed another year of seminary in order to get his Th.B. degree.

He enjoyed Baylor University's homecoming activities in November, 1909. His next trip to Texas was at Christmas when he got a new suit of clothes. But time and again he wrote of the spiritual battle he encountered with sin and Satan. "Human eyes may not see in the dark or to the depths of one's soul. I am an unworthy and weak man." He was constantly fighting the sins of the flesh without naming them. He "strives for bodily purity and mental morality." He wrote in his diary for January 16, 1910: "How long may a man keep getting up when he falls?" and again, "God may forgive a sin but its effect will curse the forgiven person til death." And "The storm is never-ending but if I go down, I will go down fighting. God help me!" Little did he know when he wrote those words how he would one day go down into the depths.

On January 24, 1910 his spirits were lifted when he received a picture post card from Jewell in China. In March he got a longer letter from her. It was only natural for a missionary on the field to write to a newly appointed missionary. Jewell, while at Baylor, knew how much letters from the mission fields meant to the students. How much should be read into Jewell's sending a picture post card and note to Carey Daniel? Evidence of a romance between Jewell and Carey at Baylor or in Louisville is lacking. She does refer to his being present when she was appointed to China. Another time he met her train in Louisville and she went with him to some preaching appointments.

Carey came up for consideration again as a missionary. On August 23, 1910, he was appointed at Richmond, Virginia. One of the first places he went upon returning to Texas was to see the W. B. Glass family who were in Kosse, near Waco, on furlough. Wiley B. Glass had served as pastor of the Mart First Baptist Church while a student at Baylor. Dr. Glass (Baylor gave him an honorary doctorate while on furlough) never turned anyone away who had questions about life or mission work. Carey's meeting with the Glass family began a relationship that carried on throughout his life.

Carey really felt like a missionary after his visit with W. B. Glass. He left Waco on the MK&T railroad for San Antonio. There he took the Southern Pacific railroad for El Paso where he stayed over for a visit with C. D. Daniel (a cousin of Rufus Daniel) in the home of Pastor Jeff D. Ray. Ray had been Carey's pastor when Carey was for a short time a member of

Waco's Seventh and James Baptist Church.

Carey sailed from San Franciso on September 20th with Charles Alexander Leonard and wife Evelyn Corbitt Leonard, on the *China* of the Pacific Mail Steamship Company. The first stop was Honolulu, then Japan and finally, Shanghai, China. In addition to Daniel and the Leonards, there were fourteen other new missionaries on board, including: C. C. Marriott and wife Cora Burns Marriott; Miss Edna Earl Teel for Yangzhou; Miss Elsie West Gilliam and Miss Louise Tucker for Shanghai; Miss Mary Alexander for Canton; and Miss Pearl Pauline Caldwell for North China.[20]

There were also returning veteran missionares on board: E. F. Tatum and his wife Alice Flagg Tatum (their China years: 1889-1914); Peyton Stephens (China service: 1893-1924) and wife Mary Thompson Stephens (China service: 1893-1942); Ella Jeter (China service: 1905-1914); and Louisa Whilden, daughter of pioneer missionaries Bayfield W. Whilden and Eliza Jane Martin Whilden, who first went to Canton, China, in 1848. Louisa's mother died in Canton in 1850. (Miss Whilden, nicknamed Lula, was the senior missionary on the voyage. She served in China from 1872-1916).

While in Shanghai, Carey and some of the others visited the First Baptist Church of Shanghai, better known as the Old North Gate Church begun by Matthew T. Yates and John Shuck in 1847.[21]

Carey and those headed for North China sailed from Shanghai on the *Koon Shing* on October 16th, and arrived at Chefoo (Zhifu), port of Yan'tai on the 18th of October. The trip had taken them 28 days from San Francisco to the northern tip of the Shandong peninsula.

Missionary Daniel spent his first week in Chefoo in the Stephens' home. After some adjustment, Miss Emma Belle Thompson, a missionary from Louisville with ten years behind her in China, met him and took him by mule-drawn *shentze* the sixty-five miles to Huangxian. Mules were often used for long trips instead of human bearers. They arrived in Huangxian October 26. Huangxian City had 12 missionaries and 12 children (seven of them belonged to the Newtons,[22] with whom Carey lived the next 18 months). Others were the

Lowes, Miss Jessie Pettigrew, Miss Jane Thompson, Miss Anna Hartwell, Williford, Charlie Hartwell (whose wife knew no Chinese and fit in China about as well as C. W. Pruitt's second wife Anna — not well).[23] Carey had an interesting note in his diary at this point: Life, he wrote, "will be long enough if lived aright and too long if lived wrong."

Jewell Legett (on left) with classmates at the Missionary Training School, Louisville, Kentucky, about 1908 or 1909.

8
JEWELL LEARNS FROM LOTTIE AND LI

Lottie Moon's last three years in China were Jewell's first three. Here is how she recorded some early "village evangelism" with the veteran missionary Lottie Moon.[24]

> Jane Lide and I went with Miss Moon one day visiting. I still see in my heart's eyes this dear old servant of Jesus stepping from one to another of the worn-out old millstones with which that street and numberless others were paved, holding her long skirts up out of the street sewage, answering the children's familiar greeting, nodding to mothers nursing their babies on the door steps, utterly unmindful of the revolting stenches all about. When we arrived at the home we were visiting Miss Moon climbed upon the brick bed, motioned Jane and me to do likewise, then induced the woman of the house and the neighbors and children also to sit on the *kang* with us. And it was there as she taught it to the Chinese that I learned one of her favorite hymns, one which countless times in the years that followed I have used, "God sees us." "*Tian-Fu pi neng kian Wae, Sheng King ming-yian shue-kwoa.*" ["Our Heavenly Father watches over us, for the Bible tells us so."]

Jewell often recounted the last time she saw Lottie Moon. It was in the pioneer missionary's home in Dengzhou (now Penglai). She told Jewell: "You must give attention to writing; writing home about China and what God is doing here." Jewell remembers how important this was that Lottie Moon said it again, "Write. Write at least a half hour every day.

Write constantly to America about the need of the people for Christ." Jewell loved to write and Lottie Moon's words encouraged her for many years to write. Sometime after that last visit with Lottie Moon, Jewell wrote in her diary:

> Nearly forty years did Lottie Moon write and work and live for China. Heartaches, heartbreaks, loneliness, unheeded appeals for those who were dying without Jesus wrenched her poor heart and at last, her fine mind. Famine, of which she had seen so much, came again horribly to Pingdu. Mentally confused, she imagined her dear friends there starving, though we were caring plentifully for Pingdu Christians. Fear closed in upon her that the Foreign Mission Board would have to discontinue its work in China. "If my people are starving," she must have said to herself, "if the Board has no money, I will not eat." Without our knowledge she refrained from eating.

On another occasion Jewel and Jane with their limited Chinese were out witnessing in the markets and temples. She recounted one of those days this way:

> Nothing is so exquisite a joy as announcing to one who never heard it that God is a Spirit, present *everywhere*. Every hill and mountain is temple-crowned in China. The Chinese believe they must go to these temples to worship. Suppose you and your Bible woman had been out to some village teaching. And as you were coming home you should meet an old woman walking with weary, aching, bound feet along the road. You fall into step and say, "Big sister, where are you going? You seem very tired."
> "I am tired, but I have fifteen miles yet to

go. I am going to Bao Derong Gian temple. Our donkey is sick. I'm going to visit the god that heals animals and make an offering."

"But your feet are bound, and that temple is high in the mountains, and the road is rocky and steep. I'm glad my God doesn't require me to make such painful journeys."

"Your God doesn't require you to? I don't know your God. What temple is he in?"

"My God is a Spirit who is everywhere, old big mother. He is here on this road with us now. He has been right with you every step you have made on this long journey. He will go with you to the temple and all the way home, and then He'll be with you to love you and care for you every minute in your home all the days of your life. He's been in your home all your life, you just didn't know it, you see. And His book says that you can worship Him right there at home, any minute of the day or night, or tell him your sorrows and joys and he's there and hears and sees. He doesn't want you to make these long, painful, useless journeys up into the mountains. They are useless, Big Sister, because the idols in the temples are just man-made things. They aren't gods. The one true God is the one I've been telling you about. He sent me here to find you and tell you about Him and His Son. His Son gave his blood to wash away your sins.

Though Southern Baptist women historically have never been encouraged to "take the lead" or preach in the churches, there were opportunities abroad for them to "preach." This was not true in every Mission Station in China but seemed to be common in the North China Mission. Some women missionaries could preach as long and hard as any of the missionary men. Among them were Lottie Moon, Martha Foster Crawford, Blanche Groves and more recently Pearl

Johnson and Bertha Smith of South Carolina.

The missionaries of the last century in North China, especially the single ones, led lives of discomfort and loneliness. There was persecution but not of a violent nature. Usually it was in being ignored or laughed at in the streets or even when trying to teach or preach. Irwin T. Hyatt, Jr., in his book *Our Ordered Lives Confess* quotes Presbyterian Julia Mateer's remark:

> Most questions have at least two sides . . . We say, "Behold these filthy Chinese, who seldom bathe or wash their clothes," and the Chinese say, "Behold these filthy foreigners — what an amount of washing and scrubbing it takes to keep them clean!"

Every year the North China Baptist Mission, as was the custom on all Southern Baptist mission fields, held annual meetings to plan and pray. Jewell's first was in the city of Yantai in 1910. She remembers this as a glorious blessing — just especially for her. The meeting that year was held in an upstairs room of the Chefoo Missionary Home. [These hostel-like homes were run for all missionaries, regardless of denomination and primarily for the families. Hotels were not very comfortable and were generally avoided, if at all possible, when the whole family traveled. When out on evangelistic tours the local inns were used.] The missionaries from Pingdu traveled overland six days by *shentze* to get there. One's first Mission-wide meeting is usually an unforgettable experience. It was so for Jewell who wrote in her diary:

> Janie, Floy and I were a tip-toe with interest, and all the folks from all the stations were eager to see the new folks — us! And when I went into the room the first time, there sat Miss Moon and beside her was one of the world's beautiful women, Blanche Rose Walker.[25] My Blanche, who joined Southern Baptists from another group, came with the J. V. Dawes.

O blessed day that ever I learned to know these three God-given fellow workers. [Note: They came to Southern Baptist work when the Gospel Mission disbanded.] Laura Dawes died in a car wreck in America in 1939.

The Pingdu famine of 1911-1912, which came on the heels of the *Xihai* Revolution that overthrew the Qing dynasty, was one of the most difficult times in the lives of the missionaries. Jewell's diary has much to say about this first famine she encountered. Jewell came to know and love one of China's most humble and successful Baptist preachers, Li Shouting,[26] who was impressed to become a Christian from the life and words of Lottie Moon and C. W. Pruitt, who baptized him.

Li Shouting was from the village of Hwoa Pei, near Shaling where Lottie Moon began the first church in Pingdu County. The Shaling Baptist Church building has been gone since before the Cultural Revolution (1966-1976) but the cornerstone has been preserved in different member's homes looking to the day the church can once again have a worship center and be reconstituted. Li, who had five brothers and began school at eight, could not stay in school because the family was so poor. Since the teacher was a friend of his father he taught Li Shouting and hoped for payment down the line. When Li was 23 he began teaching school at Shaling. In his third year teaching in the village school, Lottie Moon came to Shaling. Out of her rented home she taught about Jesus. Li attended some of her classes and later said, ". . . I thought of her as a foreigner preaching a foreign doctrine, and was not pleased — unwilling to hear or investigate. I thought this doctrine was not equal to that of Confucius, not so deep or complete. . . . I decided not to believe and to do what I could to keep others from believing — thus the door of heaven, not willing to enter myself or allow others to enter."

Finally one day after a "Jesus lesson," Miss Moon gave him a book. Li said, "If the paper had not been of such good quality and the characters nice and plain I would have burned it." He went on to say, "I put the book up out of the way on a shelf. One day, having become weary in preparing for my students, I thought of this book." He was still not willing to read the book but finally forced himself to get the book down and give it a try. The title was "The Truth Manifested." Li found the opposite of what non-believing critics of the book had told him. His interest grew as he read.

It was about this time the Lord sent C. W. Pruitt to Shaling. Pruitt explained the scriptures so clearly Li had few questions, but doubts still plagued him night and day over this "foreign religion." After taking all his doubts to God in prayer, Li confessed Christ as his savior, and he and a fellow villager, Brother Dan, went to Huangxian to study the scriptures for two weeks. The following year, Li Shouting, age 27, was baptized by Pruitt into the Shaling Baptist Church not far from Pingdu City.

Li's father immediately told him he was crazy; brothers and friends would have nothing to do with him. Because he would not worship idols nor worship his ancestors or burn paper at their graves he was persecuted, even beaten. He wondered why he had become such a problem. He said, "My faith grew weak. I thought if I am now so sorely persecuted, without cause, what will my brothers mete out to me, after the death of my father and mother, when I fail to observe the rites of ancestral worship?"

One day while pouring out his soul to God in prayer, he gained a peace that made it clear he had nothing to fear. The persecution did not let up, but his faith was stronger. His brothers were not willing for him to take off for Sunday worship. So he did seven days work in six days in order to attend the church services. Another time Li's wife overheard his brothers plotting to kill him. She immediately went to the brothers and pled with them not to be so cruel to their own brother. By doing this she had made the brothers ashamed. They thought no more of killing him. It was still three years before Li's wife professed faith in Christ and was baptized.

Lottie Moon suggested to Li that he move to Dengzhou and help the missionaries with language study. His brothers were opposed to this and refused to let him take money from the foreigners for such work. It was at this time, in 1891 that William H. Sears and his wife moved to Pingdu. Pingdu City had no church and the Shaling Church was the only church in the county. They had members in six near-by villages. He went at every opportunity to hear Dr. Sears preach, sometimes walking 15 to 18 miles to a preaching point.

Missionary Sears urged Li to consider the question of becoming pastor of four new churches in the Pingdu area. Li gave the matter some serious thought and after much prayer, "decided that if the Lord wanted me to do this, I would do my best. The year was 1899 and the four churches called Li Shouting to be their pastor and that fall he was ordained. That summer he baptized 26 converts but the following year, 1900, persecution came to Christians and foreigners in Shandong and Shanxi provinces as they had never known before. The Boxer Rebellion, as the Righteous Fists Movement is called in the West, exploded on the scene. It was based on a long-nursed hatred many Chinese felt for anything foreign. At first the Imperial troops did little or nothing to contain or stop the slaughter. Rev. and Mrs. W. D. Herring, early Southern Baptist missionaries (then with the Gospel Mission), narrowly escaped with their lives during this time.[27]

The Boxers destroyed churches and many members had household goods stolen or burned. Officials in some areas tried to force Christians to give up their faith in Jesus. Many were sorely persecuted and even thrown into prison. Some fled to port cities where it was safer due to the large numbers of British, French and German troops. Some hid in caves or anywhere they could hide to elude the men turned mad with power and hate.

Li writes, "I often had nothing to eat or drink and suffered much, but I realized it was for Jesus. His power was manifest in caring for us, and all was peaceful in the fall." When the eight foreign armies destroyed the Boxers the danger passed. Pastor Li served as middleman in arranging and receiving indemnity funds the Manchu dynasty was forced by the foreign powers to pay. Evidently his work pleased the masses as they presented him with a marble tablet and "several banners."

Along with the women Li organized an anti-foot-binding

movement and a temperance society. In 1905 Li's father died and the Christian funeral service impressed the rest of Li's family in a positive way. In 1909, the year Jewell arrived in China, Li baptized 166 new church members into the seven Pingtu County churches. In 1910 he baptized close to 300 souls. He said, "Our seven churches of Asia are at peace and God's Spirit is moving the hearts of His people to do great things for Him." It is estimated that Li Shouting baptized several thousands during his ministry in Shandong province. W. B. Glass wrote about Pastor Li:

> He is one of God's great men. As simple as a child, yet marvelously wise in directing the affairs of the Kingdom. His heart is as tender as a young mother's and in it he carries all the joys and sorrows of the 1,500 people who look to him for spiritual leading. I cannot verify it, but I am of the opinion that he has immersed more people than any living Chinese. The total numbers that he has buried with Christ in the liquid grave is now past 2,000.[28]

Pastor Li Shouting helped organize the first Chinese Baptist Home Mission Board for Shandong Baptists. This group of dedicated Chinese pastors and laymen did amazing work during the famine of 1911-12 in an area west of where the Baptist foreign missions worked. Southwest of Pingdu two flourishing churches and villages were abandoned due to the crop failures. The people scattered to the four winds begging for food. Many who were in good circumstances were left absolutely destitute. On a salary of $120. (1910 U.S. dollars) Pastor Li led a subscription for relief work with a gift of $25. About the famine Jewel Legett wrote the following home:

> Sunday the crowds here were immense. There were sixty children in my Sunday school class, many of them beggars. With the women's class present the church would not

hold the people. The children were noisy and disturbed Pastor Li Shouting, so I took the beggars, children and grown ones, out of the eleven o'clock service. I took them to the women's chapel. There were just 96 of them. I told them about heaven and how to get there, and never my whole life long will I forget those women's faces as they listened. With baskets on their arms, sticks in their hands and two or three children apiece they listened to every word.

I became pretty scared once. Beggars have done some dreadful things here of late. They have stripped women and left them naked on the road; they killed people for their grain; robbed and plundered fearfully. I hadn't any money with me. I said to them, "We do not distribute money on Sundays because we can't manage the crowds. On weekdays we distribute what we have to spare and every-day at the hospital. Go there tomorrow and Miss Jones will give you some money.[29]

They asked where the hospital was and left very quietly, which surprised me, I must say. I asked Jo next day at noon how many beggars she had that morning and she said about a hundred. She gives each one ten cash (one cash is equal to one-fourth cent American). In the city, on the first and fif-teenth of the month they may beg and it is the custom for each shop to give them one cash. They came to our home by the dozens every day to hear the gospel before they leave. Jo loves this work. She said last night with tears of joy and satisfaction in her dear eyes, "There are crowds of beggar children at the hospital every day, and they hold out their little hands to me just as if they know I'll put something in them. I've gotten so that when I'm asleep I see those little hands stretching to me from every side." Many of these beggars are *ti-mian* — aristocratic women who never in their lives begged before. Many of them were well-to-do a year ago. Many hundred thousand are starving, because of the floods of last year. Women came to our classes and bring as their only food dried sweet potato leaves or tree leaves.

Evangelist Li Shouting, colleague of Carey and Jewell, baptizing new coverts in an outdoor baptistry, about 1905. (Courtesy of SBC IMB, Richmond, Va.)

9
JEWELL LEGETT
BECOMES *LAN GU-NIANG*

Jewell loved the stream that ran beside the Pao Tsung Kian Temple just outside of Pingdu, the city where she began her missionary work. Long afterwards the memory of that restful spot remained real to her. Years later Jewell wrote to her only granddaughter, Joy, about Pao Tsung Kian.

In the letter Jewell told her that when she would have severe headaches, she liked to go out and put her feet in the stream and relax. The temple had life size idols standing on pedestals all around the big room and larger idols in the middle. Sometimes Jewell and other missionary colleagues would take a snack to eat and afterwards hang their dish cloths and dishes to dry on the altar. The incense had a sweet smell and seldom were the monks around and very few worshippers.

The fresh mountain air was healing, as was the silence. One has to be in a Chinese town or city to really know how distracting noise can be. She loved to put her feet in the water and study or read or just rest. She said once she would love to write a book about Pao Tsung Kian. The stones of the temple are hundreds of years old. "We never felt a moment of fear. No priest ever came. Sometimes there would be hundreds of people on some special *bai-bai* (worship) day and we would just stow our belongings out of sight and climb to a quiet spot and study and rest till the crowds finished burning incense and left.

While out walking one day in May, 1910, Jewell got a close up look at one means of travel she never knew possible. She told of seeing in one row nine wheel barrows with sails. "They were loaded with bamboo and the sails were all set. The caravan made a pretty sight and the squeals of wooden, un-oiled axles were terrific. One feels queer, tho, to take a seat in a wheel barrow or a rickshaw, with a human being for motive power. For a long time I couldn't, not until I realized how desperately the men wanted the work, how dire the necessity for work was theirs."

The area of Shandong province where she lived had over a million people. She said just some years ago the missionaries were the ones keeping the China postal offices in business. The six foreigners living in the area used "as much again as the natives" just six years ago. The missionaries estimated they used an average of $20 a month on postage but learned from the postman that the Chinese now use double that amount. Jewel said, "China is waking up!"

Here from Jewell's diary is a typical new experience in a Shandong village nearly a hundred years ago:

> The day we went to Chi Li Hwea-tzi some Christians met us about a mile out of the village and insisted on leading our donkeys in to the village. The dearest little lad seized my bridle. He looked about thirteen and was so brown and bright-eyed and clean that I loved him on the spot. But you can imagine how quickly I lost all desire to pat him on the head when I learned he was a married man. He had been married three years. Later when my five or six year old son, Carey, probably never knew his playmate, Wei, was married. Carey knew so little Chinese language. I never told him. Many boys were married at ten and usually to girls older than themselves who could cook and sew for them. Ugh!

In a 1910 letter she wrote to her family, friends and churches in America recounting how exciting it was to see women learning about Christ and learning they could read if given an opportunity. Opportunities for Chinese women in old China, other than raising children and crops, were rare indeed. Especially for the peasant farmer's wife. In her letter to America, dated January, 1910:

> The class for women is in session now. The one for men just closed with 27 baptized. To date 116 women have been enrolled in this

class. They have been sent here by "the seven churches of (Pingdu) Asia," to be taught three weeks by the women missionaries. They have walked from ten to 27 miles on their poor bound feet, carrying their bedding or babies. All 116 of them sleep in the Bible woman's quarters and another building in the compound. Some have had to be put on straw mats on the dirt floors. They study six hours a day.

They are taught in their quarters also. Yesterday at suppertime I went to find Mrs. Oxner. [Cora Huckaby Oxner, missionary wife of Dr. J. M. Oxner.] Passing from one row of buildings to another, I had a good opportunity to see them. They are seated on the warm brick beds, limbs crossed under them, eating cabbage and bread and drinking the tea which they had brewed in a large gourd. I like to be among them when there's somebody (American) near who can talk Chinese among them. It takes courage to face them alone. I feel like Rebekah Owen, the baby girl in our station, who returned to America only last week. She likes to go among them with her mother but when they find her alone and crowd about to feel her clothes and rub her hands, and "jabber," Rebekah gets frightened and cries.[30] I want to, too, sometimes. They love me though. They have been praying for a long time for another needed teacher. They call me their *Lan guniang* — their Miss Legett.

When I at last found Mrs. Oxner, she was seated with them on the mat-covered brick bed. This bed is a bricked-in platform running the length of the room, with the flue from the cooking stove built into it. She was teaching them Christ's Golden Rule (she said!). I sat down to learn the verse with them. One old woman drew my hands into hers and rubbed them warm, and whispered something. Mrs. Oxner translated it for me: "You must pray the Heavenly Father to help you learn our words. We pray all the time to Him to do it."

It was in one of these classes that I understood my first sentence. It was in a prayer: "Heavenly Father, give Miss Legett sense!" Mrs. Oxner hastened to explain in a whisper, "Honey, its idiom. She means understanding, ability to learn the language."

The boy children have just come out in their Easter suits. You should see them. Every boy from eleven or twelve down dressed in nothing in the world but smiles and red queue strings.

Jewell remembered seeing women come awake to the fact that they could learn — to watch a human face as its owner comes into understanding that she has a mind. To witness the pure joy of a woman as she learned a character, then two of them, three and than a whole sentence. To hear their cries of exultation as they learned that they could learn a verse of a song. There were so many Chinese women who came to realize "I am not a thing! I'm not *wooden* — [one of their words for 'stupid'] — I have a mind! I can learn!"

Then later to hear them say, "I have a soul! God loves me just like he does my man!" And still later, "Jesus died for me, just as he did for my man!" "Dear reader," Jewell wrote, "whoever you are, try to imagine the humble, exquisite joy of the missionary on this errand of awakening souls."

In those days women were bought and sold in many areas of China, especially in the farmlands and poor famine-stricken regions. China missionaries had a special term for Chinese women who many times did the work of a pastor. They could visit in the homes with women and do work with women that men were by custom forbidden to do. They were called Bible Women. On one occasion Jewell and Mrs. Giyang, a Bible Woman who became very special to Jewell, were going somewhere in a *shentze*. As they rode along they listened to the conversation of the muleteer and a man walking along the road with him. The man was trying to sell his wife to the muleteer. Jewell never got used to having women treated sometimes with less respect than livestock. But she was wise enough not to interfere with the conversation of these two strangers. So much of the missionary's burden brings them back to their knees in prayer. There is not much else they can do. But to believe in prayer means you are doing the most important thing of all.

Sometime after Jewell moved from Pingdu she lived just outside the West City Gate of Laujang City, almost beside the inns where women were bought and sold. It was a place Jewell found too horrible to describe in her diary or letters. "But oh, the joy," she wrote, "of going into one of those wretched inns and saying to one of those desperate women, 'How much were you sold for, little sister?' Then telling her of a man who was sold for thirty pieces of silver. 'He was sold to buy you from Satan. Do you want to hear that story?' It was a point of contact and one that deeply impressed these women who were treated in just as vile a way as was Jesus.

Pingdu was an appalling place to Jewell. Indescribably sordid, morbid — she had never witnessed such living and was hesitant to share it with American audiences. As Florence Jones often said to Jewell, "It's awful to be a heathen." Such a turn of phrase today would be considered not "politically correct." But in the day and time it was said it was not taken as harsh a judgment as it is today.

As an example of heathenism, Jewell wrote about Tsei Yun, a Chinese girl of 19. Tsei Yun was still a small child when her concubine mother was turned out of her home. The mother carried the baby Tsei Yun in her arms through the deep snows and the heat of summer, until she could do it no longer. She had to give the little one away and "herself to an easier, more shameful life" Jewel writes.

Little Tsei Yun, still a child, was sold to a family who sent her to her future mother in law's house. There, as was the custom, she became a slave to her mother-in-law to-be. She braided straw used to keep the fire going in kitchen and the *kang*, a brick bed, that stayed warm through the long winters.

When she was seven the mother-in-law bound Tsei Yun's tender little feet. The toes were bent under and wrapped tightly. Bones would break if necessary. A few months later they unwrapped the feet and bent them more and wrapped them again. This would go on sometimes for a year or more. The pain of such an ordeal can only be known by one who has experienced it. Never to walk again in a normal way, but only totter along and look graceful to the men. Her work continued without a pause. She would just have to crawl around to get her work done now.

Jewell's burden for such girls caused her to comment that "it is the daughters-in-law who suffer most from the heathenism of this dark land." Women had few rights in those days any where in the world, but in China they had none. They were treated as playthings or workhorses, but never for the beauty and intelligence God gave them. That would have to come later to China as it slowly has come to the Western world.

10
CAREY DANIEL
NOW *DAN MU-SHIR*

There is no evidence of a courtship beginning while Carey and Jewell were in Louisville. It is more likely that sometime after Carey's arrival in China in 1910, they began to notice each other. Both of them were out-going, never-met-a-stranger personalities. But decorum and manners prevailed to an extent unheard of today. If Jewell or Carey wrote in any detail about their love affair it has never been found. But somewhere on the plains of northeastern Shandong their attraction for each other began to emerge — or began to dawn upon these two dedicated servants.

Carey Daniel is mentioned by Jewell as being present at her appointment service in May of 1909. The following year he came as a missionary to the same Shandong province that Jewell had been appointed to serve in. In the beginning it is evident that there was little time for romancing between the two — even from the start. Carey got to China just in time for some harrowing experiences in the off-and-on revolts against the Qing dynasty rulers. No dynasty ruled China longer than the Manchus, who came south to Beijing in 1644, and defeated the Mings and founded the second foreign dynasty in history (the other was the Mongol Yuan dynasty, 1271-1368). In such a turbulent time Carey and Jewell never got around to writing about how and when they knew they were for each other — at least, to date, no written record of their courtship has been found and their contemporaries are no longer with us.

The date of October 10, 1910, Carey writes was special. That was the date of the birth of his brother's son, M. Price Daniel, Jr. This new nephew of Carey's, Price Daniel, would one day become a United States Senator and Governor of Texas. Five years later, Carey's brother had another son, William P. Daniel, who also became a governor. Price Daniel's brother "Gov. Bill" as he is known everywhere, became a leading Texas attorney and was appointed by President John F. Kenedy as the Governor of Guam. Gov. Bill wrote the Forward to this book.

In November, Carey preached his first sermon to the Chinese. It was in English and Charlie Hartwell translated to the hundred or more present. "How one's heart grows hungry to tell the story to the multitudes."

Mail took a month to get from Texas to Shandong. On November 24th, 1910 he had his 33rd birthday and first in China. The Newtons gave him writing paper and a goose dinner and a cake with candles. He used the beautiful writing paper for a seven page letter to his father that is included in this book's Afterword. This celebration was brief for there was little time away from language study. He was busy with Mateer's primer.[31] The only time he got off (except usually Saturday afternoons) was to go to the church and hear itinerant preachers such as Jonathan Goforth.

With the approach of winter Carey noted the snow — "great soft flakes fell thick and fast with a noiseless fall as pretty and gentle as the morning's dew on the flowers of Spring." With a poet's heart he went for a walk one winter day with Mrs. Newton, thereby gaining more insight into the life of foreigners in China.

His first Christmas in China he played Santa for two of the missionary families and seemed to thoroughly enjoy himself.

The year 1911 starts off almost like the land had become a deep freeze. In between language lessons and when time permitted he spent some of this winter reading a newly published missionary biography "Forty Years in China" by R. H. Graves, the South China missionary with the longest time on the field of any Southern Baptist missionary in history.

The Plague in Manchuria was easing into Shandong. Rumors of the revolution increase. Carey takes an hour out from language study each day to teach Edith and Rachel Newton arithmetic. Probably why Mrs. Newton took Carey on a walk in the snow, to corral him into teaching her girls.

The red circle around Feb. 10 came sooner than Carey wished. It was the date of his first Chinese examination. He wrote, "It will be a revelation to the examiner, Miss Hartwell, of how much I _don't_ know." Normally such tests of the missionary's language ability were scheduled throughout the year and given by an elder missionary rather than the Chinese teacher. It was thought by some missionaries that the teacher would be too easy on the student and not want to offend the student by correcting him or her. Such was unfortunate in the early years of studying Chinese, teachers were few, text books even fewer and seldom were the missionaries faced with any mistakes they made in the language due to the politeness of the Chinese.

Examination day began with his usual morning exercise and a breakfast of porridge and pancakes. It was his way of living in two worlds — the Chinese eat lots of porridge for breakfast and Americans eat pancakes.

He got Brother Newton to help him review for his test and then went into the parlor area where Anna Hartwell grilled him long and hard for two hours. She was gracious and said he had the 214 radicals down and that his writing of Chinese was in proper stroke order. She gave him a break for lunch and told him they would take up the rest of the test at three in the afternoon.

After lunch Carey asked Brother Newton to help him review for the last part of his exam. Newton immediately said no! He took the opportunity to explain to Carey that he has always refused to do any work (and studying Chinese is work) on a Saturday afternoon. That half day, Newton expounded, is sacred to recreation. He went on to say that Miss Hartwell ought to be aware of that fact!

After such a reprimand Carey was not in a mood to study so he got two of the Chinese to help him repair Miss Hartwell's stove. She had been complaining about the stove for days. He is more than ready for the test but Miss Anna informs him at the last minute the rest of the test is postponed until Monday. Evidently Newton got word to her on this vital matter. She didn't notice the stove was repaired.

Monday's delayed test evidently went well as there is nothing in Carey's diary about it. The next Saturday afternoon he and Brother Newton and Newton's mule set out for the seaside, a mere eight miles from home. Along the way the mule got loose and they spent a lot of their Sacred Day of Recreation chasing the mule through the narrow alleys (called *hutongs* in North China) of the neighboring village.

At the Huangxian River they came upon some quicksand. The village boys followed them to the river for they knew it would be some scene if these foreigners got caught up in the quicksand. And they did, Carey almost losing his shoes in an attempt to avoid the quicksand. In their preoccupation of crossing the shallow part of the river the mule got away again but this time Carey wrote, "a Chinaman caught him."[32] Much of the fun of going to the sea shore was the fresh air and getting a good salt bath. Carey makes no mention of swimming or of knowing how to swim.

The month of March brought the dreadful news of how the Plague had come to Shandong. About a thousand were reported to have died in Chefoo and 25,000 in Manchuria. Schools and churches were closed for a time, but Carey's language study was not curtailed.

"Chinese language comes, but it comes slowly," he mused. With no preaching to prepare for, he helped Anna Hartwell with her elderly father, Jesse B. Hartwell,[33] who spent half a century in China. Charlie would read to the old man so Anna could teach her class.

April was garden-planting time. If the missionary wanted to eat fresh, uncooked vegetables they had to grow them. Local vegetables, when cooked thoroughly, could not be beat, but because human waste was used they could not be eaten raw without dire consequences. Carey planted squash, pumpkin, okra, beets. Another North China treat was the home-grown strawberries.

Newton finally had enough with his straying, easily spooked mule and bought two saddle horses. Carey rode one of the horses to Long Kou (Dragon's mouth) to visit with the W. B. Glass family. He had not seen them in almost a year when they were furloughing in Texas. "Glass," Carey often commented, "is a great joy to be with."

With the coming of summer the annual Mission Meeting was a welcome change from his teaching the Newton girls, chasing the mule and trying to learn some Chinese. It was his first time to meet some of the missionaries from around the province. He enjoyed it almost as much as he had always enjoyed a Baylor homecoming.

That same summer he wrote again of his despair with the battle against sin and his struggle to be a pure instrument for God's use: "If a large black mark soiled this book every time I did evil there would be little space left for the record of things not evil. God save me from my sin. ... I did wrong today and marred the angel-kept record of my life worse than any mark can mar this book,"

July and August were spent with the J. C. Owens family at Qingdao. They and their two children down with dysentery. After Owen got out of hospital Carey went to Tai'an and spent a night on top of Tai Shan and on to Jinan. On this trip he also spent several days with C.W. Pruitt in Chefoo and made two trips to Dalian Manchuria.

There was a Dengzhou Christian Association or "native association" as Carey called it with 22 churches and 4,000 members from the area. They had baptized 1074 over last 18 months. "Good to see Baptist and Presbyterian missionary friends while there." But after his second birthday in China and still living with the Newton family, he writes, "The Newton children have the custom of spanking at birthdays, getting 34 licks from each of the six children makes me quite sore."

11
WAR IN CHINA, 1912

As 1912 approached the revolution began to become a great deal more personal. The Chinese bank of Chefoo failed and Carey lost twenty dollars gold. The American Consulate informed the missionaries they should leave the interior as the armies of the Manchu Empire and those of the revolutionaries were coming their way. There was snow on the ground and more on the way as the Glass family, Carey and the others head overland for Chefoo. It would be Jesse B. Hartwell's last time to refugee. His daughter Anna, Miss Thompson, Miss Richmond, Edith and Roby Newton on horses, mules and *shentze* trudged to Yan'tai, the city of which Chefoo was a part. Roads were bad enough in good weather but in a snow storm they could hardly be used. The *shentze* mules would sink into the mud and slush and cargo and passengers thrown into the snowbanks. The pack mules could do little better, especially if the gear had not been properly stowed on the backs.

The Pingdu missionaries, and those in the west and southern parts of the province went overland to Qingdao rather than Yan'tai as it was nearer and the roads were better.

Old pioneer Hartwell, who had fought many a battle with Chinese and missionaries would fight no more. He died in Chefoo on January 3. His son Charlie buried him in Chefoo until it would be possible to get his body back for proper burial in the city he worked in so long, Dengzhou (now Penglai). In no time there are 350 English-speaking people (100 from USA) packed into the city, fleeing the war. Out in the harbor the American cruiser, the *Cincinnati*, waits to be called on to help. The missionaries take turns leading the Sunday services and Bible studies aboard the ship. Carey finds it a blessing to spend time with these young American sailors.

When the revolutionaries are in control of Penglai and Huangxian, waving their white revolutionaries flags, the missionary men feel they must return and help with the Red Cross work in these cities. They are given revolutionary passports and Red Cross armbands in hopes they can arrive safely in Penglai and Huangxian. They take a transport from Chefoo to Dengzhou and then go overland to Huangxian. In Huangxian they estimate at least 300 revolutionaries are inside city and 800 Imperial troops outside the walls considering a counter-attack. Charle Hartwell and Dr. Ayers, with their ability in the language are able to go to work immediately with the wounded of the city. Lottie Moon had not gone to Qingdao or Chefoo when the Consulate told the missionaries to flee. Instead she was in Huangxian when Carey, Charlie and Dr. Ayers arrived. Once the men got involved she returned to Dengzhou. Carey was sent to fetch Charlie's wife at Kung Kia Tswang.

Carey learned early that there is nothing romantic about war. The real thing is nothing but terrifying. When reports come of three revolutionaries captured by the Manchus, soaked in oil and burned, his heart is heavy and his soul weighed down. On the gates of the wall are the heads of six imperial spies that the revolutionaries beheaded. The Imperial troops decide to re-take Huangxian and force old people and children to stand in front of them as they begin their attack once again on the city.

The revolutionaries are out-manned and my mid-February the Imperial troops are once again in control of Huangxian. They do not touch the foreigners but watch them closely as they minister to the sick and dying. They, as it were, "guard" missionaries and their hospital from the murderous and hated revolutionaries.

During the days of this Imperial occupation some citizens, to save their own skins, pointed out revolutionary sympathizers to the Imperial troops. One that was pointed out was beheaded without a word. Then the four soldiers started to cut off the head of the dead man's son. The boy's uncle grabbed the boy and said to the sword wielding soldiers "you won't get much money for this boy's head. Sell him to me. — I'll give you 300 cash for him." They agreed. The uncle said, "I haven't money with me but have credit at a wine shop. We will get drinks and money there." So they went and drank and drank and drank, until they were so drunk they were nearly asleep.

The uncle cut off the Imperial soldier's queues and hurried to the Imperial headquarters where he turned them in as revolutionaries, and the Imperials promptly cut off their comrade's heads unknowingly.

Then one morning, just a few days after the Imperial troops re-took the city the missionaries look out on the streets and there are no troops. The Manchu soldiers are nowhere to be seen. Fear of the revolutionaries returning in force had caused them to leave after ransacking the city.

The timing of it was fortunate for the local citizens. It was February 18th, the first day of the Chinese New Year. It was not a very happy one but it at least the blood-letting was over. Later in the month Carey wrote an article that was published in the Texas *Baptist Standard* in a March, 1912, issue, he called "War and The Red Cross in China."

With the revolutionaries back in charge of the city he and a Chinese co-worker scattered literature among the revolutionary soldiers at Bei Ma and Long Kou. Carey and Li Yong Chin visited soldiers and Pastor Tswong preached. Meanwhile they learned that in Penglai, Mr. Sen had been shot while pleading for all queues to be speedily cut. Co-workers Shin, Wong and Ting were all in danger of losing their heads. The seminary remained closed but since some students came without knowing the situation two of the teachers, Pastor Tsang and Kao Te Ching, gave classes for them.

So Shandong, like Henan, Hebei, Shanxi and the Northeast and Eastern seaboard had moved into what came to be known in China's history as the period of the Warlords. Yuan Shikai had been made president of the new Republic of China. His aim was not a republic but to restore the old dynasty and make himself emperor. His greatest problem was fending off the countless warlords who were already staking their claim to their part of China.

In April Carey has moved from the Newton's home to live with the Glass family. On April 28, As he and Glass entered Long Kou's west gate, soldiers were taking two robbers to execute them. Carey tried to talk Glass into going with the crowd to see the execution. "I wanted to see it but Brother Glass was too tender hearted. The robbers had defiant faces and manner. An excited mob of hundreds press to see the execution." Glass had already seen enough slaughter and had not stomach for any more. But it reminded Carey of the mob that must have followed Jesus procession to Calvary, only without Jesus. After long days of preaching, walking and visiting their scattered congregations he wrote: "Sleepy, but must feed horse and take a bath first."

Carey Daniel and Jewell Legett as they appeared in the 1907 Baylor University annual. (Courtesy of The Texas Collection, Baylor University, Waco, Texas)

12
"DELIVER ME FROM MY WORST ENEMY!"

May 19, 1912 was a red-letter day for Carey Daniel. He preached in the Chinese language in a regular church service for the first time. Later he writes about his feelings of having finally spoken a message he hoped the Chinese at church could understand:

> I'm very happy and very sad tonight. Before me is the possibility if not prospect of great blessing. I'm glad, too, to be able to speak understandingly in Chinese. But I'm so sad because of my sin. God will rebuke me, He will chastise me and I pray He may. Let him strike me dumb, or wreck me anyway He sees best physically if such is necessary to mold me into perfect spiritual manhood.

But it is not many pages on in the diary that he is again beset by the demons that caused him so much inner turmoil as he wrote on May 24: "God will punish me for disobedience." And on June 2 the entry seems to be almost the same: "Pastor Tsang preached to throngs by the river this morning. I have rested and sinned this afternoon." Here is a man steadfastly giving his best when at times everything seems to be against him. He wants more from himself than he can give.

It is June, 1912, that he makes the first mention of Jewell Legett since coming to China nearly two years before. It is possibly that their relationship began about then to be more than co-workers or friends. This was during a visit to Pingdu where Jewell was carrying on the work of the ill Lottie Moon. He spent over two days there, staying with T. O. and Lizzie Hearne. Lizzie Hearne and her medical missionary husband directed the Oxner Hospital in Pingdu.

As the summer of 1912 approached, the revolution appeared more and more to have succeeded in overthrowing the last of the great dynasties of China. The Manchus from the northeast overthrew the Ming dynasty by 1644 and began the longest dynasty China ever had. The early rulers were among China's greatest but by the mid-19th century the Western powers and their opium and armies had about ravaged what was left of the once proud empire.

Hong Xiuquan (1814-1864), a Hakka Chinese from Guangdong (Canton) spent three months studying the Bible with Southern Baptist missionary I. J. Roberts (1801-1871) and not being totally acceptable to Roberts' view of Christianity left and soon led one of the greatest revolts in Chinese history based a great deal on Hong's own brand of Christianity.[34] Hong Xiuquan and his Taiping Tianguo (Heavenly Kingdom of Peace) nearly brought the Qing dynasty to its knees. Now this new revolution was threatening the Manchus as never before. The leader, Sun Yat-Sen, was also a Hakka.

Carey Daniel was needed in Qingdao during July and August of 1912. The Baptist missionaries in the East Coast city, The J. C. Owen family[35] were all ill with dysentery. Carey stayed with them throughout until the parents and two children were well out of danger. After Owen was well enough to leave the hospital, Carey traveled southwest to the city of Tai'an where a couple of decades earlier T. P. Crawford had begun his Gospel Mission. Crawford had fallen out with Southern Baptists feeling too much subsidy and support was given to the churches. He felt the churches should pay their own way and take care of their church buildings without foreign mission help.

Tai'an is the nearest large city to Mount Tai (Tai Shan)[36] one of China's five sacred mountains. There he spent the night on top of the mountain so as to enjoy seeing the sun come up from across the Yellow Sea in Japan, the land of the rising sun.[37] From there Carey went to the present capital of Shandong, Jinan on the Yellow River. He then went to Yan'tai and the neighboring Chefoo for a few days with the C. W. Pruitt family. While there he found it convenient to make two trips across the Bohai (Bo Sea) to Dalian, the northeast China city in then Japan-controlled Manchuria.

He attended the annual meeting of the Dengzhou

Christian Association or "native association" as Carey called it. The pastors and missionaries attending represented 22 churches of several Western denominations with 4,000 members from the Dengzhou area. The year previous these churches had baptized 1074. Carey enjoyed the fellowship, saying how "good to see Baptist and Presbyterian missionary friends while there."

The story of Pruitt's old gardener impressed Carey. The old gardener, Carey was used to seeing around the Pruitt home, was born during the Taiping uprising. When he was born all that was left in his home after the Taiping armies rampage was a hen that laid an egg a day and the boy lived on that. As a young man with no schooling or training he was next to being a beggar. He was taken in by missionaries and given work and turned out to be a most useful friend and Christian. Carey told himself this was a lesson for him — not to judge the outward appearance.

On July 21st, using Charlie's horse and buggy, Carey took Mrs. Glass and baby W.B. Jr. and daughters Eloise and Lois for an outing. Later he bought a horse — more like a Mongolian pony — and named it Old White — the horse that stayed with him to the end.

He sadly records that on September 28th, baby W.B., Jr. died. Carey went with Dr. Glass to bury the boy in their Chefoo plot. It was on this trip to Chefoo that Carey met Ida Pruitt, daughter of C. W. and Anna Pruitt. She had just arrived from the States. She stayed a couple of months visiting her parents. The months stretched into years as Ida tried to be a missionary but her special talents in a social ministry were not as fully appreciated. She later found her calling in the Peking Medical Center. Among her gifts there was the ability to give purpose and meaning to life to unmarried pregnant village girls. There could be no greater sin to the Chinese than a girl who had known a man before marriage. Carey must have recognized her special qualities, which included a deep understanding of the Chinese women and their trials. Carey wrote in his diary how much he enjoyed knowing her by these words: "Everyone enjoyed her visit."[38]

The end of the year of revolution did not bring peace or

stability. In Huangxian alone 500 recently discharged revolutionaries, "the good guys" looted the city. They did not want to be discharged empty handed. The financially strapped new Republic had no bonuses or rewards for their soldier's war efforts. With peace returning to the area Charlie Hartwell was now able to move his father's body to Dengzhou for final burial.

January, 1913 began much more peacefully than 1912. Carey's salary is 95 Mexican dollars. Area churches he is more and more relating to are recorded as a prayer list: Chao Yuan, Shang Tswang, Teng Ki Tswang, Yang Kia Ten, Pao Ki Tswang, Pe Kuria, Chao Kia Tswang.

Feb 17, 1913 — A spell of loneliness and homesickness worse than usual comes over Carey. "I was mean in my feelings and was in condition to be naughty. Gave 35 copper pieces to Miss Dozier on her birthday." Singing at Newtons with Miss Dozier.

March 2nd writes he is tired of eating three meals a day alone. Old Bro. Kao, father of Young Kao, the seminary professor, needs to be "straightened" up and preaching again. Seems he was unjustly treated.

I Hsoa Shang not happy going to Chao Kia Tswang. The Mission has Invited Brother Morgan to work in Laiyang. Glass cut his hair and he cut Glass and Newton's hair. Blind man baptized last year cannot be used if he keeps smoking cigarettes. He wants to go to a blind school. (Yantai has one we visited in 1985). During February Carey attended a church trial. Three members found smoking opium. Those accusing and prosecuting them had a bad spirit, but may have helped.

In 1913 the Baptists were enjoying amazing growth in converts. Revival fires had broken out in Korea and spread to Manchuria, then south across the Bo Hai Sea to Shandong. There were even native Korean missionaries now coming to Shandong. Goforth's messages were scriptural and powerful. In Chefoo the preaching meetings were held in a tent that could seat 1000 people. On up the coast In Dengzhou, missionary Adams baptized 17 just during the preparatory meetings. In Huangxian, Dr. T. W. Ayers reported Goforth telling him the Huangxian meetings exceeded any Goforth had held in Manchuria, Korea or Wales. In Pingdu missionary Owen said they had never witnessed anything like this — so many coming to hear and receive the message of salvation through Christ. Cora Oxner reported she "never saw anything more real than the conflict between Satan and the Holy Spirit" as in these meetings.

In April 1913, Edgar L. Morgan[39] makes it known to the Mission that he sees a great need for Baptists to have a Mission Station in Laiyang City, that lies southwest of Yan'tai, half-way to Pingdu, one of the most responsive areas. He is willing to go there and begin such a work. Two single ladies have also show interest in going there. Carey, after visiting the Morgans about such a need and how someone should go there, is much impressed with the idea. Morgan, in the meantime, has peace about staying in Laizhou. After an always refreshing visit with the Morgans Carey walks again up Mount Tai to see the sunrise once more and spend time alone. Down the mountain he goes a bit farther south and visits Confucius' grave outside the village of Qifu. Back in Huangxian he reports to his missionary colleagues that Brother Morgan "is very happy at Laizhou" and does not feel led to move to Laiyang at this time.

Evangelistic trips into the interior and outer reaches of his Station in Laiyang and Huangxian consumes his time. He reports, "A foreigner can draw a crowd anywhere." The 1913 report shows 184 were baptized in Huangxian Station and 54 in Laiyang. He suspects the Roman Catholics of stealing sheep near one chapel at Pe Ma. In Shandong, Baptist Mission politics and differences of opinions were common as they are anytime two Baptists get together. The Mission apparently did not agree with T. F. McCrea[40] and his objections about the educational policy of the Foreign Mission Board. And the Huangxian Station recommends building a college in Huangxian. But such things are not of the utmost importance to the new missionary and his new work station in Laiyang. From October to December he commutes between Laiyang and Huangxian. Then amidst his move to full time work in Laiyang he notes: "the way is rough. Sin made it so. No one is his worst enemy but himself. God deliver me from my worst enemy."

13
THE SPRING OF 1914: JOY AND HOPE

January 10, 1914, Carey began the day-and-a-half trip from Laiyang to Pingdu and for the first time in his diary has something more to say about Jewell Legett than just that he saw her. He spent Sunday, January 11th with Jewell and wrote: "We plan to be married Feb. 25 and begin life together in Laiyang Feb. 26." The very next day they bought lot of Dr. Hearn's household goods. Then he wrote that Jewell is "the finest, purest, noblest, sweetest woman in the world giving her heart and life to a man whose heart has starved with hunger for her and whose heart is satisfied and happy within." It is one of the most positive remarks, devoid of the 'black sins' that seemed to be around every corner in his life. She was certainly what the young missionary needed. He, apparently, met the need of her heart also.

It was about this time, that Carey took Jewell up to his cabin in the hills outside the city of Huangxian. She called his hill "Dan Shan," — Daniel's mountain. She said it was a good ten miles from Huangxian and she called it Dan Shan (*shan* means mountain in Chinese) because, as far as she knew, he was the first white man to explore it. Shandong is a big province with lots of hills and great mountains. Missionaries and foreign businessmen had been in the area for over 75 years. But it is possible he was the first non-Chinese on this particular hill.

Half way up they could look through a wild ravine and see the ancient port city of Dengzhou (then spelled Tengchow, now Penglai). Another view took their breath away as they watched an eternal spring pouring itself into big bathing pools.

Carey, using the stones scattered all over the hills, had built a tiny cabin. On that particular day, she wrote in her diary:

> [He] drew me inside, closed the door, took
> off his old grey cap and pulled me into his

arms and kissed me many times. And then he said, "Girl, this is the only home on earth that I have to give you, but I'm so happy to give you this, and it is yours."

They stayed on the mountain and made plans for the coming year, the summer of 1914, when they could spend all the time they wanted together in this lovely hideaway. Her diary continues:

> I was going to give him a rest, the first real rest he had had in ten years, and he was going to love his girl for once just as much as he wanted to, to lay his head in her lap and talk without interruption from the Chinese and read to her, oh, books and books. ... But when the day came on which we had planned to start he was resting in Jesus arms and our mountain home was the refuge of desperate Manchurian red beards robbers.

The young lovers had been very discrete in all the times they had been together. Very little time did they really spend alone. It was the culture of the times. But by this time they were becoming "an item" of most of the missionaries' conversations.

But later Jewell wrote of an encounter they had sometime that year.

Carey enjoys the 1914 Chinese New Year festivities at Qingdao with Jewell. Quiet hills and singing pines of Qingdao are something they both remembered well. They mailed out wedding announcements. He tells her of his vision to carry the gospel to 1000 of the 1500 villages of Laiyang county this year. He told her too how much he had dreaded meeting with the area pastors and co-workers but it had a happy ending, "the men came and a good spirit came with them."

After the Qingdao vacation Carey is busy building a house for his bride, but he took time to write his mother that

Jewell "loves to be loved." On Sundays the workers are not allowed to work on the house but all go to church and receive half-day's pay.

On January 20th, 1914, Carey Daniel took pen in hand and wrote Dr. R. J. Willingham and Dr. Ray at the Foreign Mission Board offices in Richmond, Virginia. The young couple wanted their parents to get a telegram on the day of the wedding. Carey's request of the home office was to inform their parents on the day of the wedding. He wrote that immediately after the wedding he would cable the FMB and "On receipt of that will you please send telegrams to our parents: T. R. Legett in Port Lavaca, Texas and to G. M. Daniel, Tyler, Texas, and say to each 'Married. Carey. Jewell.' Thank you for sending messages for us. Sincerely Yours, J. C. Daniel."

On Monday, Feb. 23, Carey left Laiyang at three in the afternoon and reached Pingdu the next morning at 11:30 just in time for lunch. The wedding was at 7:15 P.M., Wednesday, Feb. 25, and S. Emmet Stephens[41] performed the ceremony. Medical missionary W. H. Sears gave the bride away and Jones and Jeter were bridesmaids. C. A. Leonard[42] served as Carey's best man. Among those present, Carey recalled later, was the Edgar L. Morgan family and their new baby boy, Carter.

Edgar Morgan loved the young Carey Daniel very much. He remembered Carey as the Shandong Mission's Texas cowboy — "riding, singing and slapping his boots with his whip."[43]

Morgan concluded that there is a great difference between a flying Texas steed and a bungling Mongolian pony, but Carey enjoyed his Mongolian mount and got as "much joy in living as anyone in Texas could. He did a great deal of evangelizing on horseback."

Morgan notes in his sketch of Carey Daniel that the Foreign Mission Board rarely sent single men to the mission field. Single women seemed to be more adaptable and could work with the local women in a way a foreign man could not. Daniel's single status caused concern among some in the Mission. Some ten years later Morgan remembered the young lovers and their wedding in this way:

In our general gatherings it was noticed that these two were reserved and seemed to avoid one another. This may have been in our mind - - or it may not. Great was our relief and warm the congratulations when it was finally announced that there would be a marriage down at Pingtu. It came on a wintry night in February, 1914, and we felt the importance of the occasion justified our making extra effort to be present. Our baby boy was only four months old and this was his first trip away from home but at his age a wedding meant nothing to him. My brother-in-law, Emmet Stephens, was the officiating minister and the wedding went off with a lot of good will. Next day the bride in a *shentze* and the groom on his horse left for their new home, the isolated station. We saw them off with our best wishes and prayers.

As the single women missionaries and wives worked overtime to make the wedding a success, Jewell enjoyed watching. The dining room was a bower of green; starred with white daisies and geraniums. The flowers, Jewell said, were grown especially by the clever hands of Florence "Jo" Jones. Also abundant were the Chinese sacred lilies and white carnations. White carnations were the class flower for their Baylor University class of 1907.

When the bride threw her bouquet, the four single ladies all had hopes, but it was Pearl Caldwell who caught it. Just about this time refreshments appeared and while they were partaking and listening to speeches from highly inspired guests, the sound of music came from outside. It was Chinese wedding music on Chinese instruments. Then an added treat appeared. None of them had noticed that Mr. Stephens had slipped out of the room, and got the school's musicians (a brass band) to come into the yard and play "Jesus, lover of my soul." Stephens then had the boys play a form of "Home Sweet Home." Pingdu was never the same after that!

83

After Jewell and Carey's wedding, Chinese and foreign guests sang God's blessings on them as they mounted the queer [Jewell's word] Chinese conveyance and left for Laiyang where no other bride and groom of their race had ever lived. Morgan expressed the joy many felt for the young couple as they began their new missionary work as a team:

> The station, Laiyang, was a day-and-a-half from anywhere. Working alone, Daniel had had a dreary, lonely sort of existence, but now with the presence of a wife he was strengthened for endurance of hardships. which seemed now to be a light thing. He went to the out-stations and little churches with hope and confidence.[44]

At sundown of the second day of their trip from Pingdu to Laiyang, Carey Daniel drew his bride close and whispered, "What do you see, way down yonder in the valley?"

Along the floor of the valley were hundreds of villages, from which the smoke of supper fires curled lazily away and nestling among the villages a crooked old city wall, within it many temples, shops, fields, memorial arches, buildings of various kinds. Outside the walls long stretches of ordered rows of over-crowded mud homes.

"That is Laiyang, dear, that is home." They rode silently on toward the land which they knew in their hearts the Lord, their God, had given them. Laiyang County, at the time, had six churches. Years later Jewell mentions the area having a "wee Woman's Missionary Society" which she most probably organized.

Carey Daniel's eyes shone, and smile never brighter, as he led her room by room through the little home he had prepared for them. How thoroughly he had made over the old native house. With the help of Chinese carpenters he had sawed coffin-lengths of logs — all lumber was cut in coffin-lengths — and made floors, foreign windows, doors, partitions and a bathroom. A native mud brick cooking space and a built-in brick bed he had torn out and put in their places real ones from Montgomery Ward.

Stiff native chairs were gone and comfy rockers from America were in inviting nooks and corners. Her own treasures of books and pictures, sent weeks before, adorned walls and tables and near the stove was her little folding organ. He had placed it there "so we can sing comfortable," he said, for he loved to hear Jewell sing. There were many wedding gifts from missionary friends in the province and he enjoyed her surprise over these for he had not told her about them.

They came at last to that holy of holies in their home, the little study. A large window that he had made took up one side of the room. His books lined one wall and Chinese Bibles, books and tracts another.

Only two pieces of furniture were in the room: a chair and an immense old Ningbo desk. Furniture from the East Coast province of Zhejiang was done with exceptional care. Carey led her to the desk and said, "Do you know whose this was?" She knew. For in the home of a friend she had seen it time and time again.

"Miss Moon's desk, *in our home!*" She cried, "How did you get possession of it?"

"I bought it last year after she died," he replied.

The desk was then over 30 years old but it still held the bright red color of the pig blood used in its making. The wonderful luster that the Chinese gave to such wood so long ago still appeared to have a perfect finish. Softly Jewell rubbed her fingers over its smooth surfaces as she recalled the times spent in Miss Moon's home.

Jewell could not take her eyes off the desk. "I was a new missionary and she tried to start me right," she mused. "Me too," he said, "I wanted her desk for you." Lottie Moon had left China less than 15 months before and Cary purchased the desk. He knew if the desk ended up on the local market it might be used as firewood or the wood used to build something else.

Over the dining room table they hung a 1907 photo of Old Main and the Baylor University campus. It was a photo taken from chapel building (Carroll Library). Jewell had it especially prepared with a white mat, framed in a beautiful brown Japanese wood. It was Jewell's Christmas present to Carey in 1913.

Often during that Spring Jewell and Carey would take their supper and go outside the city to the hills around Laiyang. After eating they enjoyed reading or talking about their American homes. While at Baylor B. H Carroll was their favorite and great old teacher. On one of their last such outings they had been reading Carroll's Interpretation of the book of Revelation.

Jewell and Carey often walked on the west side of the city wall at sundown and watched the sun sink behind the hills. They felt nearer to the loved ones in America at those times than at other hours of the day, for the rays, she wrote in her diary, that kissed them goodnight in China kissed their loved ones in America good morning.

For four months the house in Laiyang was home for the young couple. They continued their language study in order to make the name of Jesus better understood in the whole of Laiyang County.

On March 2, 1914, as they were getting used to married life, Pastor Chin Swei Ting of Huangxian and Chao Yuan came and held revival meetings in the Laiyang area.

During these days of preaching and witnessing Jewell recalled how the women at Shi Tsi Pe were forever in trouble with their heathen neighbors. It seems that three years ago, soon after they accepted Jesus, this quarrel began. A woman beaten here, a man there, this family's tree stolen, that woman pelted with stones — every kind of threat all the time, taking the joy out of life. One day during the meetings these women were in attendance. Jewell asked Brother Chin, the godly visiting minister, to talk to them, to try to awaken in them the joy of their religion. He said he would.

Brother Chin opened his Bible and smiled happily when he saw the text God had given him. Much like Jewell, Chin was one who let the Bible fall open and whatever verse stared up at them, they took it as a word from God. Jewell agreed with Pastor Chin as "how present God is in our every need."

Mr. Chin took his Bible and they went to see the women.

He told them the story of Mrs. Kao, supposedly the first Shantung convert. Mrs. Kao was not permitted to go and hear the missionaries and being a girl, she was not allowed even on the street in those days. But she found a window where the missionary was teaching and applying her tongue to the paper window, made a hole and used the peephole to see and hear. God found her there. After she became a Christian she passed through every kind of persecution. But she remained firm in her new faith. Years later her husband, so impressed with her uncomplaining attitude and joy, believed. And miracle of miracles, her father-in-law became a Christian also. All because of the kind spirit and patience Mrs. Kao showed. Mr. Kao even became a pastor and their son a teacher for many years in the Baptist Seminary in Huangxian.

Jewell did not record how the story helped the "fussin' women" but evidently it helped as no mention is made of them again. She did write in her journals that "these Shi Tsi Pe women seem to go so slowly in Jesus. We know their hardships. Day before yesterday Pa-ta-ma came to church all angry because her sister's husband had had another fight with his brother. The Larsons and I had prayer for Pa-ta-ma and I ran along over yesterday morning early to see how she was. Blythe as a bird, running over with joy she met us, and exclaimed, 'O, Mrs. Daniel, the Lord God is too good to me. Yesterday I prayed and He took my sorrow all away. I can't help it if my sister's husband fights. I needn't bear that burden. Just look at what the Lord has done for me.'"

Many happy hours were spent at Lottie Moon's desk with the language teacher. He was old and "anciety" Jewell remembered. He had the long fingernail on his little finger as was the custom with ancient scholars. He wore the queue that the Manchus long ago forced Chinese men to wear. His much wadded and padded cotton *magua* — winter coat — was also the dress for the missionaries. Nothing kept you warmer in the cold North China winters like cotton or silk padded suits. When they took on the study of the Chinese language they knew they would never graduate or complete their study. It took a lifetime of being immersed in the culture and society and new words were discovered every day. As funds were availiable most of the missionaries had language-helpers as they were called. For the most dedicated mission-ary language study continued almost to retirement.

Numerous letters were written to loved ones in America and elsewhere, and diaries were kept there. Prayers were offered for their colleagues — for the burdens were too heavy to bear and the language still unwieldy — and they were very lonely on the Shandong plains. Each evening they walked upon the city wall to watch the sun go down and could sense it rising, far away, in their native land.

Just as their life together was beginning to form, Jewell, the girl and wife later would write, "he went away, to a bet-ter home!" Carey once wrote of her as the "jewel in the prophet's breastplate." Standing before that Chinese coffin in that dank Chinese temple brought home to her that all she was now was a young widow.

14
THE SUMMER OF 1914:
GLOOM AND DESPAIR

That June of 1914 had been an exceptionally wet one for the area. The heavy rains were needed for the farms. The wet weather had never deterred Carey from his preaching rounds in Texas and they would not hinder him in China. He visited the outlying chapels and believer's homes as regular as clock-work.

Jewell knew Carey was anxious to return to her from the weekend evangelistic services that summer Sunday night in June. He was hurrying to get back to her. As she thought about it how she longed that he had waited that night for the river to subside. He should have waited. But waiting for anything was not his way. She could see him through her tear-stained eyes as he attempted to cross a river that refused to be crossed. He and his horse were swept into the raging current. Edgar Morgan, the first foreigner on the scene, recalls the events of Carey's last outing that fateful June 28, 1914:[45]

> One Sunday he was at a little church, the service was over and he had eaten his lunch, after which he started back home. A flash flood came down from the hills and the dry gullies poured streaming floods into the usually almost dry river bed, which now became a vast expanse of rushing water. The villagers near the west side advised him to wait till the stream ran down - - a matter of a few hours, but Daniel was eager to get home; they were expecting a babe in a few months. He pushed on and being a brave man, he thought he could safely take the risk. He was never seen alive again.
>
> The horse, saddled, was found next morning grazing on the near-by river bank.

Searching parties made thorough search; saddle bags were found, and later down the stream in a sandbar, with only his hand sticking up, his body was found. While the search was going on, his wife had telegraphed for some missionaries to come and help. Two men rode hard to aid her. It was felt also that she needed the presence of a woman, so Mrs. Pruitt went with all speed to be with her.

A Chinese coffin was placed in a Chinese temple to await cold weather, when the body could be taken to the foreign cemetery in Chefoo. Every station was shocked at the word "Daniel drowned." Our sorrow was profound, and all hearts went out in sympathy for the bereaved wife. We heard that she was enabled to go to the temple, stand by the coffin and say her farewell and pray.

As Jewell turned to leave the temple she wondered in her heart what was next. She tried over and over to reconcile the drastic weight that forced itself down on her life. Everything had been so wonderful, but for so short a time. Her love of life so blended with that of Carey's and their experiences so similar. Again she knew in her heart that the lifelong call to China, a call she had felt from God since childhood could not be a mistake. It could not end like this. Life was not over, of that she was certain — this was not the end — for she carried Carey's child, a very special blessing that kept her going. She made her way back to the home her beloved *Dan mushi* had built. But now, the honeymoon home she loved so much was suddenly as dark and gloomy as a tomb.

The Monday following Carey's death was the beginning of the annual meeting of the North China Baptist Mission. Jewell and Carey had looked forward to their first Mission Meeting as man and wife. All their colleagues would be there. They would see many of the Chinese they knew earlier. How she and Carey had enjoyed the other missionary children, especially Elouise and Lois Glass, who were frequent visitors to their home. Seeing them again would have been so refreshing.

At the Mission Meeting Jewell attended, as all missionaries were required to, her heart was not in it. All her dreams of China since childhood now seemed so empty and unreal. The plans she and Carey had for Laiyang and farther out west of the Yellow River disappeared as a vapor. Everything had happened so quickly. Their courtship, marriage, lovely new home and ever responding ministry was making it the most wonderful year of her life. The year 1914 was a great year until now. The new Republic of China government seemed to her in rural Shandong to be better than the despised Manchus. There seemed to be more opportunities to share the gospel. While Europe was on the verge of war in 1914 there was great peace and joy in northwest Shandong. Now the sudden death of her loved one. The father of her unborn child changed all that.

Mission meeting was a time to relax, regroup and plan for the future. To be with colleagues from distant places and catch up on all the good things that had come about and hear the latest gossip. Now, none of that was of any interest to her. She set out for Yan'tai with the other missionaries but with a heavy heart.

She was one of the main concerns of the missionaries deliberations. It became evident to Jewell that the majority of the missionaries felt she should return to America to have her baby. She was not so sure. After the shock of Carey's death she could not be sure about anything anymore. She wanted to stay but she also wanted to see her mother and father in Port Lavaca as well as Carey's family. Both families wanted her to return. She struggled in prayer about what to do.

Jewell had only been in China five years. Normal furloughs came after seven years. Before that time many early missionaries went out never expecting to return to their homeland. With two years left on her first term she felt she should stay. Yet she was expecting Carey's child and her Texas family was concerned as were Carey's family. They were naturally anxious for more details on Carey's last days and a chance to know their grandchild from the beginning.

As it turned out Jewell had little to say about the decision. The Mission recommended she return to her mother and father in Port Lavaca, Texas. Edgar Morgan would never forget the closing sessions of the meeting. He told of how the missionaries joined hands in a great circle and sang for Jewell's farewell the old favorite that always brings a tear at such times:

> When we asunder part . . .
> Blest be the tie that binds

She had never enjoyed the sea and having just lost her loved one to flood waters she did not look forward to the voyage home. As she packed for the trip she came across Carey's Masonic pin. She thought it would be useful on the trip as Masons were famous for helping their own kind. But as she got ready to get on the ship in Yan'tai for Shanghai God seemed to be saying, "who do you trust, me or the Masons?" She didn't wear it.

While in Shanghai, getting passage on a ship to America, she was tempted to get the pin out again. Once again God tenderly reminded her of his ever-watchful care. She did not get the pin out again on the voyage home.[46]

Months later, in America, she welcomed the little treasure of a son, born January 12, 1915.[47] Carey Daniel's last gift to her. She named the boy Carey Legett Daniel (sometimes she referred to him as Carey, Jr., but that was not his legal name). At this point in Jewell's diary an unknown reader of her diary added a strange phrase. This added "opinion" by this unknown reader is written as though it were a "fact." In what appears to be a woman's handwriting, the question is raised about Jewell's return to the States in 1914 to have her child. For some unknown reason this strange writer takes it on herself to say that Jewell regretted returning to the States when she did. There is no evidence of Jewell having such an attitude. Jewell, at times may have felt forced out by the North China Baptist Mission when they voted for her to return to America; while at other times she appears to be aware the

Mission action was to her benefit. She mentions more than once that under the circumstance her return in 1914 was right. There was a natural pull from her own family to return. Jewell was one who usually acted only after much prayer. Years later, looking back, she may have had misgivings about the decision.[48]

June, 1914, Laiyang, China. Possibly the last photo taken of Carey Daniel before his death. Carey and Jewell entertain two missionary kids who later become missionaries. Pictured left to right: Elouise Glass (later a missionary to China with her husband Baker James Cauthen, long-time leader of the Southern Baptist Foreign Mission Board. Much later, Elouise taught English in Yan'tai, China, 1986-87), Carey Daniel, Jewell Daniel and Lois Glass (later a missionary to China's Shandong province, Japan and Taiwan).

15
LONGING FOR CHINA

Getting through the first anniversary of Carey's death was an ordeal for Jewell. Years later she recalled it this way:

> The first anniversary of father's death. It is a late hour at night. All day long, as for many days past, the shadow of that day has hovered over me, and a great terror gripped my heart. I have been dreading the approach of the hour of his death — the watch [he was wearing] stopped at 8:25 (p.m.). But when it came, my comforter, you were lying on the bed in a great humor, clucking, blowing bubbles, kicking furiously, and looking at grandma and me with the most resist-me-if-you-can air in the world, so that grandma and I were charmed into watching. You seemed perfectly possessed with the determination to be alluring, captivating, bewitching — and when we next looked at the clock, the dread hour had passed, and you had to be bathed and put to bed. Oh, the mercy of God in giving me you, little lad!

Tragedy struck again for Jewell when a month after Carey Leggett Daniel's second birthday, Jewell's mother, Alice Herring Legett, died of pneumonia. Alice and T. R. both caught the flu during the 1917-1918 Flu Epidemic that swept through much of the Western world. Jewell's father was able to shake off the effects of the flu but never fully recovered from the loss of his Alice. His grandson, T. R. Legett, III, who was born the year after T. R. died, wrote that grandfather died of a broken heart July 12, 1922.[49]

Jewell's heart was still in China. In a piece she called "Longing For China," Jewell shared her heart with Southern

Baptist readers:

> My heart and soul turn back to China, and
> I long to go with the Hearns to those dear peo-
> ple who were always so kind to us and who
> were all I had during one terrible week. I
> believe I could do more in city evangelistic
> work there than any other woman, not
> because of my unusual qualifications, but
> because their hearts were so drawn to me dur-
> ing that week. Every home in that dear city
> was open to me when I left there. I had no
> time except Sunday afternoons, for work
> among the women during the four months
> spent in Laiyang, because I was with Mr.
> Daniel in the boys' schools a great deal, and
> had my own girls' school, but there was
> beginning to be a good interest among the
> women who came on Sunday afternoons, and
> my heart yearns to go back and work for
> them. I do not love school work, but my heart
> loves the class work and country work; it was
> class work too — that I had in Pingtu [now
> Pingdu]. If it were wise to return now, I could
> not stay in America, but should beg you to
> send me back home with the Hearns. But it is
> not wise. Because of mother's poor health and
> baby I must "bide a wee" here. The Heavenly
> Father has never given any intimation that my
> work in China is finished. Indeed He has indi-
> cated in many ways that He means for me to
> return; and so I await His good time, but not
> patiently, for in my heart's eye, I see the
> women of my little city every day and realize
> that they need me. How good that the Hearns
> can go and go now.[50]

When little Carey was four years old, it became more evident to Jewell that God still had work for her in China. She

dreamed of God's allowing her and Carey, Jr., (as noted, she often referred to him as Jr) to travel "the long, long trail a-winding to the city where his father's death had opened wide the way for Jesus."

Often in America she would recall the times she and her beloved Carey would have supper on the Laiyang city wall. They would sit between the teeth of the wall as the evening winds stirred the willows growing near the moat below. At other times, she recalled sitting on the grass looking out over their adopted city, hazy with the supper smoke of countless homes. In America the sight of the setting sun always brought to mind those quiet happy hours high above the city's dust, heat and sin. It brought into her heart a home-sickness for China.

Jewell's return to China was something she always knew she should do, yet she was filled with misgivings and spent many days praying for guidance. After five years with family and loved ones in Texas she was still filled with emotions she herself could not explain.

She loved both lands and felt a kinship with both peoples. She was now 34 years old, a widow with a four year old son.

Once she had applied to the Richmond offices of the Baptist Foreign Mission Board and had their approval she got her passport. In 1919 passports were not books as they are today but was a large document on heavy paper folded neatly into the size of an average envelope. It was good for six months.

The State Department document had a striking photo of Jewell and asked for information no longer required on passports. In addition to telling her height (five feet, seven inches, two inches taller than Carey) the form revealed the following: (1) Forehead: high; (2) Eyes: blue; (3) Mouth: regular; (4) Complexion: medium blond; (5) Face: fair and round; (6) Hair: brown; (7) Chin: regular; and strangest of all, (8) Nose: retrousse (meaning turned up at the end). There was one distinguishing mark noted: a small scar above her left eyebrow. He occupation was listed as a teacher.

At the Port of Seattle she presented her new passport to

the Consul for China in Seattle. It was approved and signed by Goon Dip, China Consul. She and four and a half year old Carey Legett Daniel sailed on the eighth of November, 1919.

A typical village scene in Shandong province, 1900.

16
SINGLE MOTHER
AND MISSIONARY

During the years she had been in the United States, China began to experience the rise of area warlords. The Republic of China's president, Yuan Shih-kai, died before he could reinstate the old dynasty. Youth were on the rise through literature and new awareness of politics. Jewell was glad to be back in China. It was evident to her that the country and people were changing fast, even in the rural, famine-ravaged Shandong hills. Much had changed in the almost five years she had been away. The Republic had weathered an attempt by President Yuan Shih-Kai to re-impose Imperial rule but his sudden death avoided more bloodshed. Warlords were dividing up the country and if not stopped would set the country back another 100 years.

None in Shandong were more glad to see Jewell than Sister Jiang, the Bible-woman Jewell felt so close to. Women missionaries generally had a Chinese woman to work with them in visitation and church work. They were called "Bible Women." Sister Jiang was 32 years old before she ever heard of Jesus. She had never seen a foreigner and knew nothing about such creatures. There were no foreigners in all of Pingdu county, Sister Jiang said. "I had never seen one. And there were no believers in Jesus in our town." She heard at the market one day that a foreign woman (thought to be Lottie Moon) had told some of the women that her God could and would forgive sins — "forgive sins for his Son's sake," she was told.

Jiang was not an educated woman, already married and with a family but the thought of having her sins forgiven was a wonderful thing. Standing there in the market her friend told her that the foreign woman said, "we could pray to her God in his Son's name."

She went home and told her sister-in-law and they both agreed how good it would be to have their sins forgiven. The more they talked about it the more they thought they would try praying in Jesus' name and be rid of their sins. But, they didn't know how. They were too determined to let a lack of knowledge about anything stop them. The would try anyway. They climbed up on the kang (brick bed common in north China farmhouses), knelt and bumped their heads to God as they had always done before the temple idols.

But they still did not know what to say. Jiang said, "sister, you say prayers, you talk." Her sister-in-law raised up from bumping her forehead on the kang and said, "No, you talk, you do the talking."

So Sister Jiang bowed, bumped her head and began to mumble that she had heard if they prayed thus their sins could be forgiven. "Old heavenly grandfather," bump again, "we hear that you forgive sins for your son's sake. We want our sins forgiven." Then a long silence and she said, "For your Son's sake." A final bump of heads, embarrassed, and confused, they sat on the brick bed as a flood of peace came over them. Jiang would later testify that it was "a peace that has lasted these 32 years, for our sins were forgiven that day."

Some time later a Chinese preacher came and taught them a hymn and little by little they came to grasp something of the foreigner's religion. But not so the husbands and family. They turned against them and forced them out of their own home. Driven from home, disowned and afraid, they wandered the streets of their village. There was no way a woman could live without a home and food.

Not knowing what else to do they decided to beg. They would stop at a house but the dogs scared them away. It seemed every gate there was a fierce dog and they got nothing to eat.

They sat down beside the road and began to cry. Between them they agreed there was nothing left for them to do but die. They were unwanted by their families, no one would take them in and for them life was over. Having their sins forgiven was proving costly.

Between them they had 500 cash (about five cents in those days). They spent 200 cash on cotton and spun it into thread, ate the seeds and sold the thread for 400 cash. They saved back a tenth as the preacher had told them about the tithe belonging to God. They bought more cotton and soon made enough to rent a small room. Their husbands were amazed at this turn of events. They continued to observe the women and seeing such a change in them the husbands eventually accepted Jesus also. They were reunited with their families.

Jewell learned that Sister Jiang's sons prospered as they grew up more enlightened and filled with hope. Now when people put them down for worshipping a foreign god they are strong enough in the faith to ignore it. Where there had been no Christian witness in years past, now there were growing churches all over the country side. Among the many who were reached in the Pingdu area of Shandong was the powerful preacher Li Shouting whose exploits and ministry has been told and re-told until it is almost legend.

It encouraged Jewell's heart that when people really seek first the Kingdom of God and His righteousness, evil and sin are overcome. She saw it in the eyes and lives of so many. Not many areas, if any, matched the growth of the Christian faith in China like the Pingdu area.

But all was not a bed of roses. In the Fall of 1920 Jewell had an encounter with what she called an obstreperous, advantage-taking male teacher in the girls school, a man most difficult. Jewell was not the kind of person that had ever had much dealings with the likes of him. She feared she had not enough courage or back bone enough to stand up to him.

Things came to a crisis one morning when he refused point blank to her face to meet his eight o'clock class. Terrified by his demeanor, Jewell fled, as was her custom, to pray. She left him flat-footed while the girls stood around to see what would happen. She later confessed that her Heavenly Father's directions nearly scared the life out of her. The Bible verse that came to her was "As the flames that setteth the mountains on fire, so pursue them with thy tempest and terrify them with the storm. Fill their faces with confusion."

With such encouragement, heart pounding to suffocation, and praying desperately for nerve to carry the thing through she went back and invited the obstinate teacher into her office. Without "a smidgen of an idea," she later wrote, "of what I said to him except that it was *li hai* to the limit." And it worked. He got to class and never crossed her again. The term *li hai* means "terrible, forceful and formidable in the extreme." The teacher came right down off his high horse, asked pardon like a gentleman and she never had a more loyal co-worker than that man after that awful day. Later she told her missionary colleagues, "But the lord and I laughed together behind the scenes, after I got over my scare."

They had not been back in China but a few months when little Carey took a heavy cold and his hearing was affected. Jewell had deafness in two branches of her family and this frightened her. His health improved but she kept a close watch on his physical condition after that.

The mission policy for Chinese schools up until that time had been to educate the children of Christian and church people. There was no way they could accept the multitudes of "heathen people" Jewell said wanted an education. It was one of the difficulties the missionary faced in trying to be open to the people they came to witness to while also being wary of those that take advantage of the situation for their own gain.

There were those that wanted to be aligned with the church and foreigners because of the power the foreigners had in extra territoriality rights. Jewell knew some "scoundrels that hide in the church." The Chinese courts had no rights to arrest or convict Christians. There were not a lot of these, but one bad apple is one too many. This was another carry-over from the 19th century Opium Wars that weakened China and turned many away from Western democracy.

She was honest when she wrote about missionary colleagues in her diary. She wrote:

> [It is] so hard to love each other out here! Someone asked a returned missionary what was his greatest problem on the foreign field and he said truly, 'my fellow-workers'! The devil knows that if he can sow seeds of discord among the missionaries the field is his. I am sure that the returned missionary gave the

101

heart-felt answer to every missionary hardest problem. The art of living together is one that must be sedulously cultivated here. Once when I just couldn't understand a fellow worker my Master said [to me from scripture], 'We beseech you, brethren, to know them that labor among you and esteem them exceeding highly in love, for their work's sake. Be at peace among yourselves.' For their work's sake!

It was important "for the work's sake" that the missionaries do everything possible to work together as a unit. Only very head-strong determined people undertook to do pioneer mission work in a land where they were not wanted and where they were forced to work with personalities not of their choosing. For the sake of the work they had to cooperate and follow closely the scripture admonition to "count others better than yourselves" and live in peace with the brethren, and "sistern" Jewell would add.

17
FROM NIGHTMARES
TO DREAMS

Jewell's work kept her away from little Carey more than she wanted. Almost from dawn to dusk she was visiting the homes of church members, inquirers and new believers. Her boy was five and Jewell felt secure to leave him with servants in the daytime while she went about fulfilling the call to share her faith with the Chinese.

"How on tiptoe," Jewell wrote, "he awaited the hour when she would return, and he might cuddle down beside her for his long bedtimes stories. His day began when hers ended. How dear they were to each other in that lovely place, she was father, mother, teacher, playmate, and he, her all."

But a little lad brought up only with his mother can often have a hard time fitting in with others. Jewell's child did not know how to play. The children had all made friends before he came and there seemed to be no place for him among them. He also had difficulty understanding his teachers. Jewell did not like to remember these days and shuddered as she wrote about them.

Jewell taught Carey three years and when the American Academy opened in Qingdao he went for three months but it was not long until she felt that place would never do for him. Betting, dancing, card playing, to her the whole bunch were not lovers of clean, wholesome religion. His playmates were Russians, Jews, Chinese and everything but Americans, of whom there were only a few. Jewell said during the Christmas holidays God put his foot down about the child's going back to Qingdao.

Warlord Zhang Zuolin (Chang Tsoa Lin) had chased Wu Pu Fu to Qingdao that fall to add to the dangers there. War was ever a possibility and the Republic of China was far from uniting the Chinese. The Chinese Communist Party was organized July 1, 1921 in Shanghai and gained footholds among many students in the mission schools. Baptist missionaries W. W. Lawton and Wilson Fielder in near-by Henan province had their Kaifeng school taken over by students. They were unable to leave the school for days. There was a new movement afoot in which the Chinese were more concerned than ever the way foreign powers were running their country. They felt betrayed by their own weak government.

Having been back in China a year she became more convinced than ever she was not giving enough attention to little Carey. Her Bible spoke to her out of the Old Testament: "They made me keeper of the vineyards; but mine own vineyards have I not kept." Once when he was a little boy and did something wrong Jewell was impatient with him and as she prayed about it, repenting bitterly she heard the Sprit speak to her heart: "You spend your strength, patience, time, life for the Chinese, but you are failing your own. You are his mother first, the missionary second." It was a lesson every missionary mother was forced to face and deal with.

While seeking to fulfill her mission one night after church services she prayed: "Is there something else you would say to me? I can bear it, Father, because you are so loving kind. Speak if there is something else." And she writes that God brought her utterly to the earth prostrate before Him with this sweet message: "Blessed is he whose transgression is forgiven, whose sin is covered." Uncontrollably she wept before her Lord. Because of his abundant love and presence in trying times. She was alone except for her son and only a widow in a foreign land can really appreciate the longings of her heart at times.

The following Sunday morning, just as her Bible class assembled, the postman brought the first mail for many days. He threw it on the table and exclaimed "There! You've every sort mail!" To the Chinese post office, clerks, stores, everything went on seven days a week. There was no day of rest or worship as in America. If the postman had mail on Sunday he brought it. But to Jewell it was the Sabbath and a busy day. Chinese New Year was approaching and much had to be done to get ready for the evangelistic meetings always held at that time. It was the one and only holiday the peasant farmers had all year and great opportunity to share the gospel with them.

As much as she wanted to go through the mail she stuck to her tasks until they were done. It was not until night was she free to take the armful of mail upstairs, and lock the door and see what God had in store for her. She had been writing home about the possibility of leaving China and wondered what the reaction might be.

A cousin from whom she had not heard in years, wrote from California asking her to stay with them if she decided to return. Enclosed in the letter was a church bulletin telling of the many victories the churches were having at home.

How Jewell wished to be in two places at once. She cried unto God until her tears were dry for revival like that to take place in Laiyang. "My heart," she wrote, "famished these seven years, for just what the home churches were seeing, I cried for it. I rejoiced and prayed and besought Him for hours to give me and us here the joys and power." Later in the margin of one of her books she remembers the Baptist revivals that shook the Shandong Baptist churches in the late 1920s and early 1930s. She was not there to see it, but she had been there to pray for it. Another time she told of a dream:

> Once upon a time many years ago I had not known the Holy Spirit and did not know Christ, I did not know him. But others were praying for His power in their hearts and earnestly wanted it. One day I lay down to rest, and dreamed I was lying by the open window in the sunlight and felt the softest, gentlest kiss upon my forehead and in my sleep I knew it was the Spirit! Wasn't that a lovely dream? Somehow it took away my awe and fear of the unknown One and made me realize that He is altogether lovable.
>
> Two years later in a foreign land a meeting was being held in which the spirit power was great and the devil's [too]. Confessions were made of sin and the devil used these confessions to bring on false confessions. All bewil-

dered I went to my room one night to be led
out of my difficulties: My Heavenly Father, [I]
do not want to hinder your work. If you com-
mand me to confess my sins before that heathen audience I will do so. The preacher says
we do not know the Spirit. Father, If I do not
know Him and if by public confession of sin
you can lead me to know Him, will you let me
not miss Him?" And in the same gentle way
as (I dreamed?) He kissed me, He made
Himself known to me, there alone, in the dark
while the others were in meeting. No more
definite, spiritual experience has come to me
than that sweet and lovely one. I went back to
church satisfied. I did not make any confession of sin.

At the annual mission meeting the furlough committee
was getting the names of those due for furlough. Jewel
remembers, "Mine was due, but I didn't want to go and the
reason being that once God had set me a watchman on the
city wall, I had run away and now wanted to stay extra years
to make up in some degree for that desertion. But many rea-
sons for and against furlough fought back and forth in my
mind and heart and I could not judge what was best to do."

Such a reliance upon prayer was the hallmark of Jewell
Legett Daniel. She knew how her father of nearly 300
pounds, who seemed so strong and powerful, yet prayed
constantly to do the right thing. She wanted to do the right
thing. Staying in China might not be what God wanted of her
in the future. She must pray it through until there is peace.

A year and a half before leaving China the last time,
Jewell tells of another dream she had in the city of Laiyang,
March 2, 1925:

I had a dream last night, a satisfying
[dream], from God. When my son's father was
leaving home on his last , fatal preaching tour,
I told him that I thought the child he had

106

prayed for every night was coming. He did not say anything, but dropped his head on my breast and glad tears bedewed my dress. By and by he prayed for the child, and went away full of gladness and joy. "You are the sweetest, dearest, purest girl in the world" he said as he mounted Old White. "Oh, you just think so," I laughed back, and he said, "No, it's so," with a farewell wave of his hand. That was the last time I saw him. How poignantly I have wished I might have gone to him and said, "There is a child!" O, to have seen his face at such news!"

And last night God let me [tell him, in the dream]. He seemed — my husband — seemed to be going here and there and yonder about the place, doing this and that little chore, in his shirt sleeves. Once he was using listerine or some such medicine in his bath and I thought, "How clean he is." After awhile night came and the lamp was lit. He was sitting by it reading. And then I went to him, knelled [sic] between his knees, and pulled his head down in my arms and whispered "Pa!" And he gave one look into my face, snatched me to him and answered, "Ma!" Isn't it sweet and deliciously funny? I never said "pa" and "ma" in my life and do not suppose he did — but my son often calls me "ma" in Chinese.

18
"NEAR BUT NOT QUITE ANCESTOR WORSHIPERS"

In 1926 Jewell Legett Daniel and her eleven year old son left China for the last time and returned to America. She was fortunate to have with her the David Bryans and the Larsons, George Herrings, the Moores and the Fielders. They arrived on board the *S.S. Tenyo Maru* in San Francisco on June 28, 1926, twelve years to the day after Carey's death. Throughout her diaries she marked this date and would make a note beside it how many years had passed since Carey's death. A cousin named May met their ship

While visiting in the home of an old college friend. The conversation usually got around to Lottie Moon. The friend asked what happened to Lottie Moon's desk. The desk Carey Daniel gave her as a wedding present.

This caused Jewell to decide to send for the desk. Back in Shandong upon hearing of her request for the desk the Chinese cut the timber to pack the desk carefully. They used mules to carry it to the docks.

When the desk arrived safely Jewell's primary concern was where it would serve the most good. Jewell remember how difficult it was to find a place to pray when she was at the Training School in Louisville and so temporarily she placed the desk in the newly built prayer room at the Woman's Missionary Training School.

In November 1929 the missionary society of Rochester, Texas sent Mrs. L. M. Ray, the president of the Texas state Woman's Missionary Union, along with the desk to the annual meeting at Beaumont. The meeting was held in the church were J. H. Pace was pastor. During one of the services Lottie Moon's desk was presented to the Texas WMU.

The next year, at the meeting of the Southern Baptist Convention, May 22, 1930, the desk was presented to the Southern Baptist WMU to be placed permanently in the Lottie Moon Prayer Room at the Missionary Training School in Louisville, Kentucky. The women of the First Baptist

Church of Amarillo sent to China for one of Miss Moon's chairs to go with the desk. Long-time Southern Baptist missionary Ivan V. Larson[51] packed and sent the chair from Shandong. The other things in the Lottie Moon room are her tea table, rice bowls, chopsticks, and scrolls; her Chinese Bible and hymn book and her cookbook with its famous Virginia recipes.

In a painting of Lottie Moon by Dr. Peter Plotkin, professor of portraiture at Hardin-Simmons University, Jewell Daniel's co-worker Bible Woman, Mrs. Giang, is seen and beside her a little girl and Pastor Li Shouting. The painting is more than 7 by 5 feet in size. Thus the prayer room felt so needed by Jewell in 1907 became a reality a generation later.

In 1927 Jewell married another Baylor classmate, John Quintin Herrin. As noted earlier, they were in the same 1907 graduating class at Baylor University. There is no written record regarding how well they knew each other at Baylor. There are few records of their student activities. Even less is known of how they came together and married when Jewell left China for the last time. After graduating from Baylor, Herrin pastored a Baptist church in Estancia, New Mexico. He had four children by his first wife. She made no mention of John Quintin Herrin to James B. Rogers when he interviewed her for the Southwestern Baptist Theological archives during the mid 1980s. Jewell seems to have felt it was a mistake that she married him. Jewell's son, Carey, was not overly fond of the man.

Carey Legett Daniel attended Baylor University. He was ordained to the ministry in the Baptist church in Baytown, Texas, on his 22nd birthday, January 12, 1937. His father before him was ordained at the same age. Jewell was in Bernalillo, New Mexico, and could not be present but sent a telegram that was read at the service. The newly ordained Daniel preached that day from the Old Testament book of Hosea.

The Spring of 1937 Carey began a church in a subrub of El Paso, called Sunset Baptist Church. There he met Jessye Burge and on February 20, 1939, they were married. Later he was pastor of the Central Baptist Church of El Paso. Jessye was born in Balwin, Mississippi. Jewell writes that Jessye was a missionary too. She worked as a teller in a bank and for years supported her invalid father. Jewel wrote in a picture album about Jessye:

> Beautiful brown eyes and naturally curly dark hair, lovely complexion, a captivating personality and a winsome sincerity that just takes you. Lovely teeth and mouth; full of pep and life and fun, and a business woman to her toes (with the prettiest little feet!)!

Carey and Jessye named their daughter Esther Joy Daniel. Joy, born August 30, 1943, earned a B.A. degree at Baylor University, her grandparents school, in 1965. After teaching school a year, as her grandmother Jewell had done before her, she became a nurse. Joy is married to Randolph "Randy" Martin. They have three children, Michelle, David and Suzanne. Michelle and Suzanne are fourth generation Baylorites. Carey Legett and Jessye Burge had one son, Carey, Jr., who did not survive, he was born and deceased July 31, 1945.

In 1903, one of several churches that Carey helped to organize while he was at Baylor was the Bowman Grove Baptist Church, near Waco. (The church that broke away from the Center Church in Hill County during Carey's pastorate.) On May 17, 1953, Carey's son Carey L. Daniel, accompanied by his mother Jewell, preached the 50th anniversary sermon in the church. Jewell writes that there were still twenty-one of the charter members still there and Carey's photo was still on the wall of the church.

The last forty years of her life Jewell lived mostly in the Dallas, Texas, area. Blanche Rose Walker, who went to China with the Gospel Mission in 1905, and became a close friend of Jewell's was instrumental in Jewell's concern for the Jewish people. Jewell writes about this, in her own hand, in her copy of Walker's biography, *Following the Leader*.[52]

Jewell loved to write even more than she loved to read. In her papers, saved by her grand daughter, Joy Martin, there are handwritten notes in old diaries, pocket notebooks, large classroom notebooks and just loose sheets. Whatever was handy, Jewell wrote on it. One of her copies of *Daily Light*, a book of scriptures for every day of the year, has notes finely written all around the margins, top, side and bottom. Most of the notes are of other scriptures she is reminded of, while others are memories.

In many of her diaries and in *Daily Light*, Jewell would romanize the Shandong Chinese characters and express herself in that way. This Shandong form of writing Latin letters for Chinese characters is no longer used. In her copy of Walker's book she would note Walker's use of the Wade-Giles' romanization of Chinese and put in her own Shandong spelling.[53]

Jewell's concern for the spiritual welfare of the Jewish community became as much a prayer burden as her earlier work among the Chinese. She enlisted groups of girls in her church to help her mark favorite verses in small New Testaments that she would give to Jews.[54] She notes in her Daily Light, 1959, she took up the burden for the Jewish people. In the summers of 1960-61, 1967 and 1968 she was active teaching in Vacation Bible Schools.

While still a student at Baylor she evidenced an interest in reaching Jews for Christ. When she was a student at Baylor University, the campus Foreign Mission Band had speakers to share their work in many areas of life. One was a coverted Jew. His words probably remained in Jewell's heart and evolved in her latter years in active ministry among Jews.

Jewell died four months short of her 107th birthday, April 18, 1991, in a nursing home in a Dallas suburb. For many years this last home of hers had a huge portrait of her hanging in the foyer which is now in her grand daughter's home. She welcomed strangers and was always ready to share what God had done for and with her in her fruitful life.

Some years before her death Jewell Legett Daniel was proclaimed not only a Daughter of the American Revolution but a full-fledged member of the United Daughters of the Confedercy. This came her way from her mother's side of the family, grandfather William G. Herring. Jewell's nephew,

Tom Legett (Lt. Commander, retired) and William Nicol (Major U.S. Air Force, first cousin on her mother's side), did the research. Jewell called them "near-but-not-quite ancestor worshippers."

Jewell Legett Daniel and her son, Carey Legett Daniel, Texas, 1915

19
"THERE IS NO SORROW
IN HEAVEN"

Soon after Jewell, the expectant mother and widow, reached America in 1914, she took pen in had to try and express something of her feeling of loss when Carey died. She would write about the ordeal again and again during her life. Jewell, who loved her Lord and the ministry he had called her to, wrote in the November, 1914, issue of *The Foreign Mission Journal*:

> So often it is said, 'Words are empty at times of bereavement,' but they are not. The Heavenly Father has used His children marvelously in getting to me the messages He wanted me to have. Ever since the telegrams began coming to Laiyang from the outside world, the Father has seen to it that His children's words have been the words I needed, and from China, Japan, America — many, many letters have come and I am thankful for every one.

Such comfort came early and often to Jewell. But it could not erase or even sooth the painful memory of losing so suddenly her only true love. Carey was her college classmate, her missionary colleague and beloved husband. Each phase of their brief life together became greater to her throughout her long life.

Years after his death she tried to write the story and could never bring herself to complete it. In the Afteword of this book is one of these attempts. Joseph Carey Daniel's passing was never far from Jewell's heart and mind. She also wrote what she could remember about his funeral service in the heat of summer in their home courtyard.

The day of his funeral, Friday, July 3, 1914, she was not physically able to attend the service. The city officials would not allow the body in the make-shift wooden casket into the court yard. Those who had come to help find Carey's body, W. B. Glass, Newton, McCrea and Anna (Mrs. C. W.) Pruitt went ahead with a service. The students and teachers from the boy's school were in attendance as well as a few of the local Christian believers.

Jewell was lying just inside the window of her bedroom and could hear W. B. Glass' remarks about her husband's life and ministry. She could hear every word. He spoke in the Shandong dialect he had been working in for more than a dozen years and when he finished he asked if Dan shiniang (Mrs. Daniel) had any words for the school boys and friends.

From deep in her broken heart, Jewell wrote out a few lines and sent them out to W. B. Glass, who translated it for the mourners. This is how she recorded it later in her diary:

> There is no sorrow there [in heaven], or parting. We can go to heaven if we trust Jesus' blood to wash away our sins. If we do not see you pupils here on earth again, I hope that Mr. Daniel and I will meet every one of you in heaven.

20
PRECIOUS PROMISES

Jewell had many favorite Bible verses. Many of them came from Paul's letter to the Philippian Christians. She wrote in her diary and I would suspect in many a letter that "If you want an elixir of life, for the sunset half of it, Philippians cannot be excelled. ... Try it under any circumstance and taste the full sweetness of our Father's love."

Almost every verse of Philippians is good to memorize. Precious promises on which she placed her life.

> "I am confident of this very thing, that He who began a good work in you will perfect it until the day of Christ Jesus: (1:6).

> "And I pray, that your love may abound still more and more in real knowledge and all discernment, so that you may approve the things that are [best]" (1:9-10).

> "For me to live is Christ" (1:21).

> "Have this attitude in yourselves which was also in Christ Jesus" (2:5).

> "Our citizenship is in heaven" (3:20).

> "Rejoice in the Lord always; again I will say, rejoice!" (4:4).

> "I have learned to be content in whatever circumstances I am" (4:11).

> "And my God shall supply all your needs according to His riches in glory in Christ Jesus." (4:19).

Jewell's only granddaughter, Joy Martin and her husband

live in Allen, Texas. She knew Jewell as well or better than anyone during the last years of her life. She was gracious to write from her personal memories in the Afterword.

Governor Bill Daniel, nephew of Carey Daniel and elder of the Daniel family, was kind enough to write the Foreword to this biography. His great love of Texas and Baylor University to which he has given his life was born the year Carey died. Though Governor Bill never met Uncle Carey you can see from his words in the Foreword of his love and respect for Carey.

Following are three Appendixces, two of them "In their own words" by Carey and Jewell. One of Jewell's stories is published for the first time and the other is a letter from Carey to his father in 1911.

Though a hundred years have passed since God called Carey and Jewell to China, God is still calling for Christian friends to share their experience with the Chinese churches and pray for God's continued blessings on their growth. A growth that these two young missionaries helped to begin in the China province of Shandong.

Joy Daniel Martin, granddaughter of Jewell and Carey Daniel.

Afterword

by

Joy Daniel Martin

Granddaughter of Jewell and Carey Daniel

When I was little, she was just a tall, shy woman I called "Moremommy." She lived several hundred miles away when I was born. So when my mother tried to explain to her toddler what a grandmother was, she would say to me, "It's like having more of Mommy." That's why I called her Moremommy.

My paternal grandmother Jewell was nearly sixty years old when I was born. Her childhood had preceded the explosion of Twentieth Century technology. Her family had traveled across Texas in a covered wagon and, as a matter of fact, she had seen only one automobile before her first missionary journey to China. She never drove and, to my knowledge, never watched a TV show. She would look up in childlike wonder at skyscrapers and airplanes almost like an alien first setting foot on Earth.

Her various residences were sparsely furnished - all old pieces - and her material possessions were modest. "Meager" might be more accurate. The one thing she did have in abundance was reading material: old books, new books, journals, devotional books, magazines, religious tracts, etc. On the foot of her bed (which, unless she was in it, was always made) were current issues of Life Magazine, Time Magazine, The Reader's Digest, The Baptist Standard and a worn black Bible. She frequently commented on the Life Magazine covers painted by Norman Rockwell and would study them in detail with great fascination.

My earliest memories of her residences were rented rooms in East Dallas homes. When I was thirteen my parents and I moved from the church parsonage to a community in a much better school district. The church my father pastored,The First Baptist Church of West Dallas, was in an impoverished area of

117

Dallas near the West Dallas projects. There were no paved streets or indoor bathrooms when we first lived there, and many of his church members could not read. The man who collected and counted the offering each Sunday signed his name with an "X". Late night sounds of police sirens were not uncommon. Though the parsonage had had a bathroom installed by the time we moved out and Moremommy moved in, this was the environment in which she spent her last four-teen years of independent living. With her perfect grammar, precise penmanship and ladylike manner, she seemed some-how out of place in this setting.

Moremommy spent an incredible amount of time on the telephone - not talking, but listening. When I would occasion-ally spend the night with her, most of her evening would be spent listening on the phone. I would be annoyed that she wasn't playing with me. Now in retrospect I realize that her most endearing quality was the art of listening with intense interest and attention to whatever someone was telling her. When talking to you in person she would make full eye con-tact, lean forward a little and have you stop and clarify any point on which she was unclear. She was in essence an unpaid neighborhood counselor. I don't recall that she dispensed advice, only that she would respond with comments like "Our Heavenly Father knows how much you're hurting," or "Have you gone to our Heavenly Father about this?" Yet somehow this intense listening and suggesting God as the answer seemed to attract dozens if not hundreds of souls in distress to unburden their hearts to her. And she, in turn, used these opportunities to witness for "our Heavenly Father," which was her term for God. Jesus was often called "the blessed Savior." The lesson to be learned from this approach is that perhaps we would be better witnesses if we talked less and lis-tened more.

Thinking back now, I wonder what personal sorrows Moremommy would have confided to an older, wiser confi-dant when she was a young missionary. Would she have said, "I miss my mother and father terribly and I won't see them for seven more years." Or perhaps, "Why would God allow my husband to drown when we'd been married for only four months?" Or maybe she would have asked, "How can I be both mother and father to my little boy and still fulfill my call to be a missionary to the Chinese?" Having trusted God to bring her through such incredible hardship had made her a compassionate confidant.

Moremommy appeared to me to be relatively unconcerned with her living environment. Having fine clothing, furnishings, food or entertainment was not a priority. Almost everything she owned was given to her by loving friends. She accepted these gifts so graciously and with such delight that people loved to help her. She had many faithful long-term friends whose financial and material assistance enabled her to survive with only a small annuity from the mission board. Neither did she seem concerned with her physical well-being and, if she ever went to a doctor, I'm not aware of it. I do recall her having chronic back pain which she relieved by standing with one arm supported on a crutch. Once we came back from Louisiana to visit her in the hospital not long after she went into the nursing home. She lay in bed with an IV in her arm and an uncomfortable looking nasogastric tube in her nose. When my husband and I asked what was wrong with her, she said she didn't know. Then we asked what the doctor thought the problem was, she said, "I didn't ask him."

My impression was that earthly life for her was just someplace to be while preparing to be united with her Heavenly Father. Her detachment from physical and material things might be compared to that of a child who, enroute to Disneyland, pays little attention to the motel room his family stays in overnight.

Unable to return to China, Moremommy turned her ministry to God's chosen people. I recall several close Jewish friends of hers who had accepted Jesus as the Messiah. The girls in our Girls' Auxiliary (G.A.'s) would sit around her big table marking Bibles for Jews. At this table would be long lists of Jewish names and addresses. The G.A.'s, as well as other helpers, would mark in the New Testament verses that were fulfillment of Old Testament prophesies concerning the Messiah. The "marked" Bibles would then be sent out to names on the list.

As a school-aged child, I was aware that people in nice cars would come to take her to speaking engagements. She could tell spellbinding stories about China that would capture the listeners' attention, and then she would make her plea for her Jewish ministry. I wonder how this very shy woman learned to deal with the stage fright of public speaking.

If one word could best describe Moremommy, it would be the word "focused." As a little girl she felt called by God to spread the Good News of Jesus and I never knew her to lose sight of that call. The last twenty years of her life (ages 86-106) were spent in nursing homes. Four, to be exact. Until well past her 100th birthday I remember her saying to various nursing home workers, "Tell me, what does the name 'Jesus' mean to you?" Sometimes she would be met with a blank stare, but frequently the workers' faces would come alive with their love of Christ, and a quick friendship would ensue between children of God.

At the age of 100 she was still ambulatory. I remember accompanying her as she walked slowly down the hallway. When we entered the nursing home dining room, two separate groups from Christian women's' organizations, each unaware of the other's plans, had showed up at the very same time to give her a 100th birthday party. Two separate sets of gifts - two sets of balloons - two big cakes each with 100 candles - two separate "camps" staring at each other. After a few awkward moments, everyone was able to laugh about it and join forces to give this little centenarian a spectacular event. Jewell "memorabilia" lay spread out on tables for viewing. There were momentos from China, letters, pamphlets she had authored, a 1907 Baylor yearbook with graduation photos of Jewell and my grandfather Carey - all evidence of a life well spent. What a spectacular moment for her! She looked so tiny in the seat of honor in front of her cake (cakes). When I was a child she was nearly six feet tall. By age 100 she had shrunk in height by almost a foot.

Moremommy adored her only child Carey. And I was his only child. Perhaps the hardest thing I ever had to do was go to the nursing home and tell her that he had died suddenly of a brain hemorrhage. We sat on the edge of her bed for half an hour while she cried and thanked God that he had been saved and that she would see him again someday in Heaven. My mom and daughter and I sat there with her until she fell asleep from sheer exhaustion. After that I never heard her mention his name again.

At the age of 103 she fell and broke her hip or, as she put it, her hip broke and then she fell. She lay in terrible pain for several days because no surgeon thought she could survive anesthesia. Finally we found a brave orthopedic surgeon and a brave nurse anesthetist who agreed to surgically repair the seven fractures under epidural anesthesia. She came through the surgery with flying colors.

The next day as she lay in her hospital bed surrounded by traction bars, she looked up at the TV her roommate was watching. Sheriff Andy Taylor and Deputy Barney Fife were talking to a prisoner behind bars in the Mayberry jail. She got the traction bars and jail bars confused and became very agitated because she thought she was in jail (remember that she was 103, had never watched TV and was heavily medicated). When the episode was over this 103-year-old woman, who was not wearing her glasses, read aloud the credits as they scrolled across the screen. She was blessed with phenomenal vision all her life. It was during this hospitalization that I first saw her not wearing her dentures.

During those days in the hospital as I sat by her bed, she told me repeatedly how thankful she had been to have a granddaughter and three great-grandchildren. I began to realize how unlikely it may have been that I and my children ever did exist. Widowed two months into her pregnancy with my dad, she had survived the ordeal of finding my grandfather's body and burying him. She had endured the difficult trip across China to the seaport as well as several weeks at sea. Then she traveled from San Francisco to Tyler, Texas, where she gave birth. What a miracle that her pregnancy survived those obstacles. It was only as an adult that I could fully understand why people loved her so. Hers is proof of what one life can accomplish when focused on the Creator. The 92nd Psalm says:

> The righteous will flourish.
> Planted in the house of the Lord.
> They will still bear fruit in old age,
> They will stay fresh and green,
> Proclaiming "The Lord is upright:
> He is my Rock."

Jewell attends wedding of her granddaughter, Joy Daniel Martin to Randolph "Randy" Martin, June 14, 1965.

Appendix I
In Their Own Words

The towns and villages of Texas in the 1880s are mostly memories today. Some of those memories can be re-lived along the Brazos River on the Baylor University campus. This is because Carey Daniel's nephew, Governor Bill Daniel, and his wife Vara, moved an 1880s village, lock, stock and barrel, from their land near Liberty, Texas, to Baylor University. Named for them, the Vara and Bill Daniel Village, is open to the public and annually thousands of school children get a glimpse of what life was like in Texas more than a hundred years ago.

Walking the dusty streets of the town, now completely reconstructed as it would have been in Carey and Jewell's childhood, frontier Texas comes alive. The village is often the site of reunions of the Daniel families.

In 1924 Jewell wrote a short story based on her experience of visiting the place where Carey drowned. She called the story "Swing Low, Sweet Chariot." As far as is known this story has never been published. Original in The Texas Collection, Baylor University, Waco, Texas. From the many notes, diaries and letters Jewell wrote it is evident she wanted to write a book of her life's experiences. Laine Scales's 1994 University of Kentucky dissertation "All That Fits a Woman" leans in that direction. The following may have been a beginning or portion of writing her memoirs.

Swing Low, Sweet Chariot

by

Jewell Legett Daniel

Lazily, crazily, the mule-litter swung along the narrow mountain path with the gentle motion of a cradle, on rough terrain violently, with the up and downness of a salt shaker or with a teeth-cracking corn popper twist. This was the North China Pullman, the country's "most aristocratic method of slowcomotion," with speed limit never exceeded, three and a half miles an hour. Sometimes by foolishly hurrying foreigners dubbed "Miz Noah!" The long passenger, missionary mother on her way to bring her small son home from school in a distant port city, groaned, "Swing low, sweet chari-u-u-t," and wished for tomorrow, which would bring her to the end of the journey and to the child.

"I'm very thirsty," she called to the "follow-a-foot man"— muleteer. "Please buy me a cucumber." Receiving no answer she listened intently and heard a voice from far in the rear. She peered through the small opening in the back curtain and discovered the driver snatching a whiff of opium from his pipe.

She knew the Chinese saying was right and to the mules she remarked, "all muleteers should be hanged." The muleteer with expertly aimed pebbles and expertly spat epithets guided the mules along the tortuous path. "Good remote control," she observed, "a pebble on the nose means 'gee' and one on the flank means 'haw' and one on the side means 'giddap.'" With resignation she re-arranged the pillows at her back. "It's sometimes up and sometimes down," she murmered as the mules stumbled along the rocky way. Then she lay back on the pillows to watch the changing view.

She loved these journeys, in spite of the body-racking method of travel and the danger of the bandit-infested mountains. The roving bands of robber-soldiers when, as now, there was the occasional flare-up of antiforeign feeling. She never tired of the quiet villages along the willow-strewn

124

rivers. She liked to find the numberless giant 'faces' which the mountains silhouetted against the blue skies. On this day she particularly enjoyed the flashes of gold and white sunlight from the floss being unwound from countless immense boiling pots of silkworms, and time and again, though grateful for the earnest hospitality of the people, smiled refusal of the bowls of silkworms offered her to eat.

An old Buddhist temple came into view, and her thoughts turned to the time when her son's father, before the son was born, had been swept away by a flood from the mountains. She remembered with poignant homesickness how he and she, married so short a time, had ridden horseback over these mountain roads. "Here!" she recalled, "We sang at the tops of our voices and rode at a gallop. "Ye banks an' braes o' Bonnie Doon," she said whimsically, "how can ye bloom sae fresh, sae fair, since that day! We sang "There's a tavern in the town," too, and "I wish I was in the land of Dixie."

The joyous young husband had gone to the country one day to visit the churches, and the flood came without notice as was common on the Shandong plains. Etched in fiery memory still was the lonely gray horse with the water-soaked saddle. The servant saw it first and her terrible cry still echoes in her heart, "Here is the horse but where is pastor Daniel!" The grueling days of searching for the body with neighbors and townspeople showed a tenderness that countered the other horrible memories. The concerned, drawn faces of loving fellow missionaries, reminded her of those who helped her through the ordeal. Because of the flooded earth Carey Daniel had had to be buried temporarily in an old temple, and she had gone away to wait for his last gift, his little son.

Suddenly the muleteer was beside the litter. With tense excitement and desperate profanity he hurried the mules and laid shaking hands on the poles to steady the conveyance. To his passenger he said only one word, but it was enough. "Soldiers!" Courage dried up in her. Soon, heavily armed, the soldiers were crowding past casting what seemed ugly looks at the foreigner and envious looks at the good mules.

She knew the driver's terror: too often were his animals commandeered, the muleteer taken to care for them and never heard from again. And what might happen to her!

"Will the inn be full of them when we arrive?" She asked in low tones. "Yes," he said tersely.

Quietly she made preparation for the stop. She ate plentifully. Fearing she might have needed to. She knew that once the inn doors closed behind her anything could happen. The animal and driver had to be fed and rested and there was no other inn along the way. They arrived finally and she saw with misgiving that the yard was full of soldiers. With a very quiet and a very frightened muleteer she passed into the mud-walled and mud-filled compound.

"Every room is taken," the inn-keeper whispered as he helped the driver lift the litter down, "and I dare not ask them to give up one."

"Oh, I beg you, give me a place where I can close the door and be out of the sight of these soldiers," she pled.

"There is no place for you at all, except the open cart-way to the rear of the buildings," he said, "there is a bench you can sit on." He was a nervous inn-keeper, afraid of what might happen to this foreign guest.

With an unnecessary word to the driver to hurry the feeding of the mules she went to the car-way and took her seat in full view of the soldiers.

Outwardly calm, inwardly hoping, she opened a book and pretended to read, but through her mind were racing stories of missionary tragedy in just such circumstances as these, and her heart was full of concern for her terrified driver. The moments seemed like hours. Her pounding heart pressing the breath out of her body. When he paused before her she lifted her head and said, "Well?" And tipping his cap in the most approved western style, he said, "I thought you would like to know, Mrs. Daniel, that you have a Christian brother in this crowd."

"Oh, who are you?" she cried, and he answered, "I was one of the guards of pastor Daniel's body while it was in the temple. I've been a Christian ever since." With a smile he continued, "I wake you up every morning. I'm the soldier

126

who blows reveille from the city wall. Also, my niece is in your girl's school and my nephew is in the boy's school."

The men with him were not stragglers, robber-soldiers. They were from her own city, stationed in the temple grounds where her husband's body had lain. Their looks had not been malevolent, but just very curious about the foreign devils and their un-Chinese ways. So, presently, she climbed into the litter and was lifted again upon the mules, leaving the inn a much humbler Christian than she had ever been, with a steadier and wiser muleteer.

Sketch of Carey Daniel in Baylor University Roundup Annual. (courtesy of The Texas Collection of Baylor University)

Appendix II

In Their Own Words

Carey Daniel's letter to his father, Rev. G.M. Daniel of Tyler, Texas
September 20, 1911

Dear Father,

One year ago today we sailed from San Francisco. The time has gone by at a rapid rate. The wheels of time never roll backwards. We are constantly nearing the end of life and are each day further than ever before from life's beginning. Its a far greater blessing than riches wisdom or honor to have time behind us well spent in humble faithful service

Each one of us struggles for himself with God as the friend and helper of those who trust Him. Yet each one is helped or hindered in life's battles by each one he meets. We cannot understand our own experiences but know ourselves better than we know any other person. I have been a dull and slow student in the school of life but am learning some things. Observation and experience are great instructors.

No man in the world has influenced my life as much as you have. In many ways you are my ideal man. I never knew you idle nor did you ever represent a bad cause. You never betrayed a friend. Strangers have found shelter under your roof. If all the good teaching you have done, the good books put among the people and all the service you have rendered was done in Jesus' name, how much our Savior has blessed humanity through you as His agent. If in doing for others we do it to Him how often your Savior has had service at your hands. It is not a theory, Thank God, but more real than the material things about us. The things of the spirit are the real things. Your heart and love has been with Christ and your feet and hands have followed your heart.

You may have grown impatient sometimes. John the Baptist who had publicly proclaimed Christ as the Son of

God grew impatient in prison and sent to ask Jesus if He was the One who was to come or should they look for another. God's providence's are God's leadings. These providence's may take us other ways than our heart prompts, but what the Lord saw of evil for us down the way He would not permit us to go was such as to justify Him in sending the overruling providence's which did come. I can almost see God's hand lifting you here, pushing you there and protecting you at yet another place. Did you dream, when as a youth of nineteen years you waded the snow with frozen feet back from he front of war, God would give you so useful a life as He has? God has been good to you and in so doing has blessed multitudes of others. You are not the man you were thirty-four years ago when into your little humble home on Big Lake Creek there was born a baby boy. You see the world different to the way you saw it then. You have seen many bad things, but more good ones than bad ones. You have had misfortunes and troubles and sorrows but would you say they have outnumbered or out-measured your blessings? God blessed you with many children that through them you might be a blessing to the world through your old age and beyond. You loved your children and later your grandchildren, so God has taken some of them on to greet you welcome by and by. None of us honor our parents or our God as we should, but God will help us all to do better; and if we fail partially or utterly the fault will not be yours. The prize isn't in the winning but in the struggle. You have been in the conflict and struggle all these years but God will give you increasing peace and joy as you draw ever nearer the time and place of perfect peace.

It was a joy to you outweighing a multitude of troubles to see Jonetta graduate. Bro. Glass was telling me a day or two ago of how happy you were in Waco. I can see you with Ira Joe in your arms talking with President Brooks or with Mr. J. C. Taylor or looking with swimming eyes when Zonetta stepped forward to receive her diploma.

Your letter of August 17 reached me yesterday, September 19. I can't think of Lee and Iva without their baby nor can I of Ira and Joie without theirs. Their hearts are young and tender and the going of the little one hurts them in a way it doesn't you, and yet they will be beyond its reach sooner than you will. I know your heart and how this child had you spoiled quite as much as you had him. And so we come once more to the grave — that place where always we must walk by faith and not by sight. Death, we discover, is real. But, thank God, no more real than the resurrection. The trumpet will sound some day. It will be glorious if we be found watching. My heart is hungry to preach. I'm not home-sick at all, but would surely like to see you all. Its only six years not till I will come to see you.

There are many interesting things in my recent experiences but I can't write them now. It was sad to me to lose two whole months from language study, but duty called and kept me. I'm in perfect health and am putting in good time on my books now. Kiss my dear mother for me and tell her I love her as I did long, long ago.

Your affectionate son,

J.C. Daniel
Hwanghsien, China
September 20, 1911

Appendix III

Carey's and Jewell's Family Heritages

I. Carey Daniel's Family Heritage

General Francis A. B. Wheeler, great-grandfather of Carey Daniel, fought alongside Andrew Jackson and William Henry Harrison. In 1823, Wheeler resigned from the Army and joined Stephen F. Austin's expedition to Texas. Wheeler's daughter Ann (born: 1829) married Allen Lowery, eleven years her senior, a still young veteran of the Texas war for independence from Mexico.

Allen Lowery became a well-known and respected minister and was a charter member of the Baptist Convention organized at Anderson Grimes County, Texas in 1848. This was a forerunner of the present Baptist General Convention of Texas. Ann and Allen had four children, the last of whom they named Sarah Elizabeth, and when relatives later learned of her birth, they requested she be given a third name of Virginia in honor of her grandparents who emigrated from that state. Virginia Lowery was to become the mother of missionary Carey Daniel.

Lowery became a chaplain with Company A, Texas State Troops, when the Civil War broke out. About this same time George Mayfield Daniel of Floyd County, Georgia, although only 16, enlisted with Company E of the 17th Alabama Regiment. After the war the Daniel family moved to Texas.

George Mayfield Daniel, whose father had also fought for the South in the Civil War, and Virginia Lowery were married January 20, 1870, in Dacus, Texas. They were the parents of Carey Daniel, missionary to China.

George Mayfield Daniel or "G.M" as he was commonly called, was born January 27, 1846, at Macon, Georgia. He died June 18, 1918, in Tyler, Texas. Virginia Lowery was born October 21, 1849 and died January 3, 1931, in Tyler, Texas. They are buried at Willis, Texas. G.M. helped build 12 churches and for 16 years was Moderator of the Evergreen Baptist Association in Southeast Texas, while pastoring several churches in the area. The G.M. and Virginia six sons and four daughters are:

Edward Bunyan	1870-1950
Lee Allen	1872-1917
Georgia Ann	1875-1934
Nissi Susan Virginia	1876-1963
Joseph Carey	**Nov. 24, 1877- June 28, 1914**
Rosa Emma	1880-1905
Marion Price	**1881-1937 (father of two governors)**
Emmet Graves	1885-1902
Ira Link	1887-1939
Zonetta Almand	1889-1972

Missionary Carey Daniel seldom used his first name, known always as "Carey." His younger brother, Marion Price Daniel, was the father of two governors: M. Price Daniel, Jr. (1910-1988) governor of Texas from 1957 to 1963. The governor is buried at Liberty, Texas. William P. Daniel, known everywhere as "Gov. Bill" was born in 1915, the same year as missionary Carey's son, Carey Leggett Daniel. "Gov. Bill" was appointed governor of the island of Guam by President John F. Kennedy. He is the author of this book's Foreword and lives in Liberty, Texas.

Missionary Carey Daniel's one son, named Carey Legett Daniel, was born January 12, 1915, in Tyler, Texas.

Carey Legett Daniel married Jessye Burge February 20, 1939, in El Paso, Texas. Jessye was born January 7, 1905 in Balwin, Mississippi. They had two children: Esther Joy Daniel, born in El Paso, Texas, August 30, 1943 and Carey L. Daniel, Jr., born and deceased July 31, 1945, also in El Paso.

II. Jewell Legett Daniel's Family Heritage

In 1880, Kernie K. Legett and Mintie Berry Legett of

Monticello, Arkansas, migrated to Buffalo Gap, Texas, just south of Abilene. Their son, **Thomas Riley (T. R.) Legett,** born Dec. 12, 1854, and died July 12, 1922, was the father of Jewell Legett Daniel.

William and Betty Herring of Llano, Texas, also moved to Buffalo Gap, Texas, in 1880. Their daughter, **Alice Herring,** born September 25, 1864, and died February 13, 1917, was the mother of Jewell Legett Daniel.

T. R. Legett and Alice Herring married September 12, 1881. T. R. was a preacher known for going to more neglected areas to preach.

Their first child, Jewell, was born in 1884, in Buffalo Gap, Texas.

The second child had the same name as Jewell's future husband: Carey Legett (1887-1978). Judge Carey Legett attended Baylor University and got his law degree from the University of Texas. Married Anne Alice Hunnicutt May 2, 1917, in Marlin, Texas. He was inspired to become a lawyer from his uncle who was a prominent lawyer and early supporter of Hardin-Simmons University. Carey Legett was a humble man whom some said was "too nice to be a lawyer." Their children: Dr. Carey Legett, Jr. (1918), Robert H. Legett (1920) and Rosalis Legett Crockett (1927).

The third child was T. R. Legett, Jr. (1892-1971), married Ruby Burns, January 26, 1921 and started first shrimp and oyster canning plant in Corpus Christi. Their children: LCDR Tom R. Legett, III (1923), Dr. Martin P. Legett (1924) and Nancy B. Legett Collis (1927).

III. Descendents of Jewell and Carey Daniel

Jewell's and Carey's son:
CAREY LEGETT DANIEL (January 12, 1915 - August 19, 1987)
    Married Jessye Burge on February 20, 1938

Granddaughter:
JOY DANIEL MARTIN (August 30, 1943)
    Married Randolph M. Martin on June 14, 1965

Great grandchildren:
MICHELLE MARTIN RESTER (April 4, 1967)
>Married James Trever Rester on August 11, 1990
>**Great-great grandchildren:** Thomas Martin Rester (December 11, 1996); David Robert Rester and Amy Katherine Rester (twins) (Dec. 29, 1999)

DAVID RANDOLPH MARTIN (March 28, 1969)
>**Great-great grandchildren:** April Allison Martin (April 19, 1993) and
>Jacob Stephen Martin (February 3, 1997)

SUZANNE MARTIN EISENBERG (June 18, 1971)
>Married Toby Matthew Eisenberg on May 21, 1994
>**Great grandchild:** Nathan Matthew Eisenberg (November 19,1999)

Sources for family heritages:

1. "Mr. Texas" by Eugene W. Baker, Baylor University booklet honoring Gov. and Mrs. Bill Daniel, pp. 47-48. Personal interviews with Daniel family members.

2. *The Shifting Sands of Calhoun County, Texas*, Calhoun County, Texas. Historical Commission, George Fred Rhodes, Chairman; Dana K. Burke, Book Committee Chairman. Port Lavaca, Texas. (1981)

3. Interviews and conversations with Joy Daniel Martin, granddaughter of Carey and Jewell Daniel.

Reference Notes

CHAPTER TWO

1. — "Origin of Mission Volunteer Band" by W. B. Glass, page 2. Baylor University, Texas Collection. W. B. Glass became a leading pioneer Southern Baptist (SBC) missionary in north China.

J. Frank Norris later, as pastor of the First Baptist Church, Fort Worth, Texas, became a leader of the fundamentalists wing of the Southern Baptists Convention. Norris once shot a man to death in his church office in Fort Worth. He eventually left the SBC, condemning it as too liberal and worldly.

2. — H.H. Muirhead, born in Eagle Springs, Texas, December 19, 1879, graduated from Baylor University in 1904 and Southern Baptist Theological Seminary, Louisville, Ky., with a Th.D. in 1923, with his wife, Alyne Guynes of Calvert, Texas (a 1905 graduate of Baylor University), spent 40 years as SBC missionaries to Brazil.

3. — From China: C. D. Morris, Julia Meadows, W. B. Glass, Jewell Legett and Carey Daniel; from Mexico: J. H. Benson, W. R. Allman, Lena Hopkins, Elouise Shimmins; from Uruguay, B. W. Orrick; from Brazil: H. H. Muirhead, Ben Rowland, F. M. Edwards, the Charles Stapps; from Portugal, J. J. Olivera; from Africa: B.L. Lockett; from Cuba: Van B. Clark.

4. — *The Baylor Line*. February, 1985, page 44. Personal interview with Jewell by Mary Calvert, celebrating the hundredth anniversary of Jewell's birth. Article has excellent photo of the eldery, but bright and sharp, Jewell Legett Daniel. Jewell's father's letter written to her on her first birthday recounts this dedication.

CHAPTER THREE

5. — G.M. and Sarah's ten children: Edward Bunyan, 1870-1950; Lee Allen Daniel, 1872-1917; Georgia Ann, 1875-1934; Nissi Susan Virginia, 1876-1963; Joseph Carey, Nov. 24, 1877-June 28, 1914; Rosa Emma, 1880-1905; Marion Price, 1881-1937 (father of governors); Emmet Graves, 1885-1902; Ira Link, 1887-1939; and Zonetta Almand, 1889-1972.

6. — *A History of the Baptists of Hill County, Texas* by J. C. Daniel was published at Waco, Texas, June, 1907 by Hill-Keller-Frost Printers. There is a copy of this book in the Texas Collection, Baylor University. Among the photos in the book is one of the young Carey and one of his parents.

7. — *The Baptist Standard*, December 14, 1911, page 20.

CHAPTER FOUR

8. — "A Plea for Christian Education" in tract form was an attempt to enlist cooperation from the six Baptist schools in Texas and their supporters in seeking patronage, financial aid and students. The six schools in 1897 were: Baylor University, Female College (now Mary Hardin-Baylor at Belton), Howard Payne College at Brownwood, Decatur College at Decatur (forerunner of Dallas Baptist University), Burleson College at Greenville, East Texas Institute at Rusk (later Industrial Arts Academy for Girls). In 1905 Goodnight Academy at Goodnight and Canadian Academy at Canadian joined the group and offered studies for freshmen students.

9. — Carey's classmate at Baylor and Southern Seminary was Taylor Crawford Bagby. T.C. Bagby was born May 29, 1885 in Rio de Janeiro, Brazil, to pioneer Southern Baptist missionaries, the W. B. Bagbys. T.C. and his wife Frances Adams, of Virginia, went as independent missionaries to Brazil in 1914, the year that Carey Daniel died in China. They became SBC missionaries to Brazil in 1918.

CHAPTER FIVE

10.— Lettie Spainhour was born in Virginia June 30, 1884, and was a public school teacher before going as a missionary to Jiangsu province, China. In 1916 she married Peter Wilkerson Hamlett who was a China missionary from 1905 until his death in 1947. Lettie retired in 1953.

11. Jane Wilson Lide was born February 25, 1883 in Darlington, South Carolinia. She went to Winthrop, College and became fast friends with Jewell at the Training School.

12. — Some of Jewell's Baylor classmates were also appointed to the mission field. Dr. Basil Lee Lockett, of Vernon, Texas, and his wife Josie Still of Henderson, Texas, were appointed to Africa. Mr. Van B. Clark, tenth son of pioneer preacher Rev. A. Clark, of Bell County, Texas, went to Mexico. V. B. Clark had felt called to missions while a student at Baylor University. He worked his way through school and was aided by the sacrifices of his father. Clark was ordained in May, 1905, by the Seventh and James Baptist Church, Waco, Texas, and appointed July 15, 1909. Mr. Davis was not appointed due to the poor health of his wife, Ellen, who died not long after the appointments.

13. — Martha was the wife of T.P. Crawford who went to China in 1850. T.P. broke with SBC and formed the Gospel Mission in the 1890s. Martha Foster Crawford evidently was loved by the Chinese far more than her impulsive and sometimes overbearing husband. There is a marble plaque to her honor in the foyer of the Little Crossroads Baptist Church in Penglai to this day.

14. — C. W. Pruitt, a farm boy from Georgia, studied at Southern Baptist Theological Seminary and was in China from 1881-1936. His first wife, Ida, was Presbyterian. They met on the ship going to China and second wife Anna Seward (China service: 1888-1936) was the mother of Ida Pruitt (that's right, she was named for Pruitt's first wife!),

social worker, author and favorite translator of the famous Modern Chinese writer, Lao She. The Ida Pruitt papers reveal that the Pruitt home was one of the few missionary homes Lottie Moon enjoyed visiting. Ida Pruitt served in the North China mission from 1912 to 1920. Her books, based on women she knew in Shandong and Peking, give insight into the plight of women in China during the first half of the twentieth century. "A Daughter of Han" and "Old Madam Yin," were published by Stanford University, 1945, and reprinted in 1967.

CHAPTER SIX

15. — Jessie Pettigrew was born in 1877 in Virginia. She studied in Chicago at the Northern Women's Baptist Training School, became a registered nurse, went as SBC missionary nurse to China in 1901. March 13, 1916 she married Shandong missionary Wiley B. Glass. His first wife Eunice died April 13, 1914. Wiley Blount Glass was born in Franklin County, Texas, September 4, 1874. Graduated from Baylor University in 1901 and Southern Baptist Seminary in 1903. He went to China in 1903. Baylor honored him with a D.D. in 1919. He was imprisoned by the Japanese, 1942-43. He and Jessie retired in 1945. For more on W. B. Glass see the book *Higher Ground*, by Eloise Glass Cauthen, Nashville: Broadman Press, 1978.

16. — Floy White taught school before going the Woman's Training School and on to China in 1909. She and her husband Wayne Womack Adams were married October 28, 1909. They both worked in Shandong and Dairen, South Manchuria (now Dalian in Liaoning province.) Floy and Wayne retired in 1943.

17.— Ida Taylor served in China from 1905 to 1924.

18. — T. W. Ayers was born in Georgia in 1859. T.W. and Minnie's son, Sanford Emmett Ayers, was born in Huangxian, Shandong, Dec. 19, 1899. Sanford Emmett Ayers

and his wife Willie Bennett returned to China as second-generation medical missionaries.

19. — Dr. Thomas Oscar Hearn and his wife Lizzie Penn Hearn did medical mission work in North China from 1907 to 1925.

CHAPTER SEVEN

20. — The years of China service for these were: Leonards, 1910-1940, when they transferred to Hawaii; Marriotts, 1910-1940; Teel, 1910-1943; Gilliam, 1910-1912; Tucker, 1910-1921; Alexander and Caldwell, 1910-1947.

21. — Yates, and his wife Eliza, were one of Shanghai's first missionary couples of any denomination. He died in Shanghai in 1888. Shuck and I. J. Roberts were Southern Baptist's first missionaries to China, having gone to Southeast Asia and Macau, on China's border, before the Opium Wars and the opening of China. They worked in Canton, China, and areas north of Macau years before the SBC organized in 1845.

22. — William Cary Newton (b. 1873; China service: 1902-1939) of North Carolina and Mary Woodcock Newton (b. 1876; China service: 1902-1939) of Rochester, New York.

23. — China service for these: Clifford Jackson and Julia Martin Lowe, 1910-1948; Pettigrew (later the second Mrs. Glass), 1901-1945; Anna B. Hartwell, born in Dengzhou in 1870, was a North China Mission member from 1892-1940; Mary Davis Williford, 1901-1936; and Anna's brother, Charles "Charlie" Norris Hartwell, born in 1884 in San Francisco, taught in China from 1909-1927. The Hartwell's father, Jesse Boardman Hartwell served off and on in China from 1858 to 1912. He was widowed thrice (Elizabeth H. Jewett who died in 1870; Elizabeth's sister, Julia Jewett who died in 1879; Charlotte Norris in 1903).

CHAPTER EIGHT

24. — Charlotte "Lottie" Moon (1840-1912) is by far the most well-known name among Southern Baptist missionaries. The annual Christmas offering for foreign missions is named for her. Because she was such a good writer, and wrote a lot, more is known of her. Hardly tipping the scales at a hundred pounds and in height a fraction under five feet yet in God's eyes she was a giant. She was born in Virginia and went to China in 1873. Something that has been lost in the Lottie Moon story are the very qualities of leadership which set C. W. Pruitt and her apart from most other missionaries. After Lottie Moon's experience living among the Chinese in Pingdu, she stopped thinking of herself as wiser and better than the Chinese, the basic Christian premise that drove many missionaries to China. She no longer joined in other missionaries' comments about Chinese dullness and stupidity. In fact, she rarely congregated with other missionaries, with the possible exception of the Pruitt family. (This fact came from an interview with Ida Pruit biographer, Dr. Margaret King, Nov. 1994.) Lottie Moon and C. W. Pruitt developed the greatest SBC evangelistic center on any of the Southern Baptist mission fields with the able help and leadership of the Chinese pastor, Li Shouting.

25. — Blanche Rose Walker was born in Fairfield, Texas April 23, 1876 and studied at Howard Payne College and Baylor University. She worked from 1905-1910 with the Gospel Mission and was appointed by SBC FMB to China July 5, 1910, working with the Interior China Baptist Mission in the ancient capital city of Kaifeng until retirement in 1938. Miss Walker traveled to the Mission Meeting with Rev. and Mrs. Joseph Vedale Dawes who was from Auroraville, Wisconsin. He was born Feb. 28, 1871 and studied at the Baptist Indian University in Oklahoma, Southern Baptist Seminary. The Los Angeles Baptist Theological Seminary gave him a D.D. in 1941.

26. — In missionary reports and FMB records Pastor Li Shouting's name was spelled several ways. A picture of him in the February, 1911, *Foreign Mission Journal*, says in the caption his name is "Levi Sheo Ting." Other times it is spelled "Li Sheo Ting" or "Li Shu Ting." His family name of Li is one of the most common in China.

27. — See *Papa Wore No Halo* by Susan Herring Jefferies on the life and times of the two David Wells Herring families. John F. Blair, Publisher, Winston-Salem, 1963.

28. — "From The Shantung Baptist Association" by W. B. Glass in the *Texas Baptist Standard*, December 28, 1911, page 5.

29. — Matilda Florence Jones, missionary from 1907-1943. She was born in Billings, Missouri, Sept. 15, 1876. She was superintendent of nurses at the Oxner-Alexander Memorial Baptist Hospital in Pingdu from 1923-1941. The Oxner-Alexander Memorial Baptist Hospital was built in Pingdu in 1907 and dedicted on April 10, 1910. This medical work was begun due largely to the work of Dr. James M. Oxner, M.D., who with his wife, Cora Huckaby, began a clinic there in 1903. After his death it was named for him. The name Alexander was added in 1923.

CHAPTER NINE

30. — This is the daughter of missionaries Jesse Colman Owens and Rebecca Miller Owens. Jesse came to China in 1899. Rebecca Miller, the following year.

CHAPTER TEN

31. — Calvin Wilson Mateer, 45 years a Presbyterian missionary in Shandong province. He arrived in China in 1863 was known for his scholarly work in Chinese and English. His Mandarin Chinese language "primer" was used widely by missionaries in North China well into the twentieth century.

32. — The use of "Chinaman" has long since been recognized as a derogatory term.

33. — Jesse B. Hartwell and T.P. Crawford were not well suited as co-workers. Often Lottie Moon had to come between the two as they disagreed over the smallest of things. See Hyatt's book "Our Ordered Lives Confess."

CHAPTER TWELVE

34. — For best English insight into the Taiping years see Jen Yuwen's "The Taiping Revolutionary Movement" Yale University Press, 1973; and Jonathan D. Spence's "God's Chinese Son" W. W. Norton, 1996.

35. — Jesse Colman Owen served in China from 1899 to 1911. His wife, Rebecca Miller Owen, served from 1900 to 1911.

36. — "Shan" is the word for mountain in Chinese. Five mountains in China are considered more sacred than others. Tai Shan or Mt. Tai is considered the most sacred.

37. — The Chinese call Japan "Riben," which means "origin of the sun."

38. — Ida Pruitt wrote two fine books about Chinese women she knew personally: "A Daughter Of Han" and "Madam Yin". She was also the favorite English translator for China's master storyteller, Lao She [Lau Shaw] (1899-1966).

39. — Edgar L. Morgan, b. 1878- and Lelah May Carter Morgan, b. 1878- went to China in 1905. They are the parents of Carter Morgan, b. 1913- appointed a missionary in 1948 to Hawaii and later Hong Kong.

40. — Tully Foster McCrea and wife Jessie C. Read McCrea were SBC China missionaries from 1904-1934.

CHAPTER THIRTEEN

41. — Silas Emmett Stephens and Irene Mouring Carter Stephens were China missionaries beginning in 1904. Emmett died in 1926.

42. — Charles Alexander Leonard and wife Evelyn Corbitt Leonard were missionaries to China from 1910-1940. One of his encouraging and informative letters on missions helped many students in the States become more interested in missionary service.

43. "Sketch 77, Carey Daniel," by Edgar L. Morgan archives courtesy of his son Carter Morgan, Westminster, S.C.

44. —Ibid. Morgan, Sketch 77

CHAPTER FOURTEEN

45. —Ibid. Morgan, Sketch 77.

46. — She kept the Masonic pin planning to give it to her son but he grew up with a distaste for "secret societies" and she never gave it to him. It went to a relative who was a Mason.

47. — The report in the official Southern Baptist Foreign Mission Board publication, *The Foreign Mission Journal*, January, 1916, p. 208, reported in error that she had a baby girl. "Mrs. J. C. Daniel has felt compelled to tender her resignation as a missionary of the Board. Her terrible experience in the drowning of her husband last year made it necessary for her to come home. The care of her *little girl* makes her return to the field very difficult." Italics by the author.

Sometime later the Daniel family in South Texas bought a beautiful organ and had it shipped to China for a memorial to Carey.

48. — The diary insert reads: "Jewell always said she made a mistake in coming home to have her son but his family insist-

ed. Some believed it was his uncle or a close relative that was governor of Texas." The person who wrote this in the margin of Jewell's diary is unknown. The time it was written is also unknown. It is unknown what relationship, if any, the person may have had with Jewell. What is known is the writer was not familiar with the Daniel family. It was Carey's nephews, not uncles, that forty years after his death were governors. Price Daniel (1910-1988) was governor of Texas 1957-1963 and is buried in Liberty, Texas. William P. Daniel, born in 1915, the same year as Carey Leggett Daniel, was Governor of Guam in the 1960s. There is no evidence the parents, brothers or sisters of Carey had any influence on Jewell's return to America to have her child.

CHAPTER FIFTEEN

49. —*The Shifting Sands of Calhoun County, Texas*, Calhoun County Historical Commission. George Fred Rhodes, Chairman. Port Lavaca, Texas, 1981

50. — The Foreign Mission Journal, April, 1915, p. 299.

CHAPTER EIGHTEEN

51. — Ivan V. Larson was born in Hannibal, Missouri, Feb. 20, 1889, graduate of University of Louisville and Southern Baptist Theological Seminary. He and his wife, Edith Drotts Larson, went to China in 1919. Edith was born in Kansas City, Missouri June 15, 1888. He was interned by the Japanese and repatriated in 1942. They completed their missionary work in the city of Chiayi, Taiwan.

52. — Jewell took Blanche Rose Walker's manuscript to Buckner Orphan's Home in Dallas and helped edit it for publication in 1957. A second edition was printed in August, 1959.

53. — In Henan province, where Blanche Rose Walker spent most of her years, the Wade-Giles system of writing was

144

more common. Today in China a more standardized form of using the Latin alphabet to write Chinese is called *pinyin*. Pinyin is closer to the Mandarin sound of Chinese than other such systems and is used by the newspapers of the world and the United Nations except in some famous historical people or places, such as Chiang Kai-shek and Sun Yat-sen or Canton or Hong Kong. In Taiwan the government continues to use the Wade-Giles method.